EARTH

Frank Townshend

THE BOOK TREE
San Diego, California

First published 1929
George Allen & Unwin Ltd.
London
Alfred A. Knopf, Inc.
New York
All rights reserved

All new material & revisions
© 2018
The Book Tree

ISBN 978-1-58509-375-5

Cover art © by
Aleksander Mijatovic

Cover layout
Paul Tice

Published by
The Book Tree
P O Box 16476
San Diego, CA 92176
www.thebooktree.com

We provide fascinating and educational products to help awaken the public to new ideas and information that would not be available otherwise.
Call 1 (800) 700-8733 for our FREE BOOK TREE CATALOG.

Contents

Introduction 7

I. THE EARTH 9

II. VISION OF THE EARTH 51

III. LIFE 67

IV. THE STORY OF THE EARTH 173

Here is my life :
All that I found on earth,
All that I did,
All that I am,
All that I know and feel.

INTRODUCTION

This book is a celebration of the earth and the beauty of life. Much like his other book, *Heaven*, it is written in poetic verse but reads more like a story. It shares powerful insights which have inspired one reviewer to call it, "the most important book ever written about mankind and our relationship to all things." I was already familiar with *Heaven* and knew how special it was—but now *Earth* became a priority. This same reviewer stated, "there could be no greater service to humanity if a publisher would make his books available." The Book Tree agreed, and has answered that call by reprinting at least two of his titles.

The author, Frank Townshend, was a philosopher, poet and prophet. After fighting in World War I he found it necessary to spend seven years in India on a spiritual quest. After this, he wrote his books. In *Earth*, he maps out his observations of the world and then shares visions of a hopeful future for humanity. He ridicules the current world philosophy based on material profit, but refuses to be regretful for mankind's situation. He states that all people, all religions, and all thought, are in their proper places in the evolution of the earth. He foresees a coming age that will be the natural outgrowth of the necessary past and the necessary present, in which life will be based on the joy of existing, and every person will find the truth in their own heart. This book foreshadows a shift in mankind so powerfully, and illustrates it so clearly, that one cannot help but to begin experiencing it for themselves.

Paul Tice

I
THE EARTH

THE EARTH

⟨ 1 ⟩

I WANDERED about the earth, meeting all sorts of people;
And I lived in every kind of place,
Doing all manner of work.

⟨ 2 ⟩

OF the people that I met, only one was completely and unalterably happy.
Indeed I observed that most of them did, whatever they did, because of fear;
Fear of life, or fear of death,
Or fear of after life or after death.
So that they piled up possessions if they could,
Hid from sight their personal affairs,
Covered their risks by reasonable precautions,
Denied their inmost longings,
Or became deeply religious or even thoughtful.

⟨ 3 ⟩

AND some men lived in hope;
Hope that was fear reversed.
They hoped for increased riches,
For perfection or salvation,

For health, fame, knowledge, or power,
For love or for amusement, for work or for rest;
They hoped for their country's prosperity, and for their family's virtues,
For an easy passage,
And for a more abundant life in the world to come.

‹ 4 ›

The most contented were those that worked with unquestioning devotion,
Yet even their satisfaction appeared uncertain;
For many who had known the joys of creation and success,
Came at last to wonder whether their work was of value.

Only the inhabitants of Africa seemed to have caught something of the happiness of children.

‹ 5 ›

In the towns people looked anxious and tired;
In the country they were aged from unending toil.
And there were many who passed their days in idleness,
Or in objectless lives of ease.

‹ 6 ›

In general, the actual makers, getters and creators of things were poorly paid;
So that labourers, cultivators, miners and artists received but little.

While people who became channels of exchange and communication were highly rewarded;
So that ambassadors were unusually well housed,
And purveyors of goods, banks, railways and steamship companies
Made large profits.

‹ 7 ›

MEN and women spent much time discussing news and politics,
Or in gossiping about their neighbours.
Not a few picked holes in our most sacred institutions;
While others hastened to support whatever was new—as long as it was new.
And there were old men who chuckled over dirty stories,
And old ladies who did not.

‹ 8 ›

SOME people overflowed with knowledge,
Others were dull, their minds the slaves of convention,
Or of arbitrary ideas of right and wrong.
Most saw evil in a number of things.

Some who feared public opinion, the law and their own bodies,
Nursed unacted desires.
Others were an outrage to all decency,
And were locked up.

⟨ 9 ⟩

Some men were satisfied with their doings, and with themselves,
Others struggled continuously to adjust themselves to the life around them.

Enthusiasms were common and contagious;
Evenness of humour rare.

⟨ 10 ⟩

People were for ever looking for guidance,
And there were enlightened gentlemen who told them every day, just what they ought to think.

There were old folk who talked of what they had done in their youth, which was gone;
And young folk who spoke of what they would do in a future, that never came.

And many, who thought they knew the truth about how to reform the earth,
Were most anxious to spread it abroad.

⟨ 11 ⟩

In their relations with each other, individuals thought mostly of themselves.
Even those who fell in love, were prepared to make every sacrifice

To get what they wanted.
And there were few who were able to forego as little as their own opinions,
For the sake of their adored ones.

⟨ 12 ⟩

SOME men occupied themselves collecting money for good works;
Still more raised funds for projects understood to be of a profitable nature.

Many spent their surplus dividends in open charity, and were publicly rewarded;
Others gave anonymously, and felt virtuous within.

Some devoted their lives to the service of humanity, and to the improvement of the condition of the less fortunate;
Others contended that there were classes of labour, doing essential work, which could not be paid adequate wages,
Because there were no profits to be made.

⟨ 13 ⟩

SOME men collected silver and glass and Japanese prints,
Because they liked them;
While others collected bottles and rags and cigarette ends,
To make a living.

And there were those who gave huge prices for pictures,
    books and antiques,
And were proud to own them.

⟨ 14 ⟩

LIFE was bound on every side by conventions.
Entertaining and hospitality crystallised into set forms;
And fellow creatures even asked each other to meals
Because they felt it was their duty.

⟨ 15 ⟩

IN many countries the beginnings of sexual life were thought
    to be unclean,
And sexual practices among the young were treated with
    sympathy, justice or severity.
For it was believed that they could be cured by kindness,
    fairness or harshness.
And it occurred to few that the ways of nature are not to
    be corrected,
But rather to be understood.

⟨ 16 ⟩

IN some parts of the world numbers of men and women
    passed lives devoid of intimate friendships;
And women died unmarried, or without bearing children.

In Europe, prostitution and perversion walked abroad,
Their faces tortured by misunderstanding or suppression,

By fear or by excess.
In the East, sex was not degraded.

‹ 17 ›

PEOPLE became uncertain about the bonds of matrimony.
And there were those who asked:
Is marriage a failure?
Commonly happy beginnings were followed by a carelessness in relationship, which fast grew to friction or boredom;
While sometimes individuals who were physically and mentally unsuited to each other,
Found themselves tied together for life.
Unfaithfulness became so widespread as to excite but little remark;
And there were influential men who publicly advocated living in sin.
Again and again married couples only held their homes together for the sake of the children,
Or as a matter of convenience.
But I met a few who said that marriage was a great success,
And who advised me not to put it off
Until too late.
The proportion of divorces increased.

‹ 18 ›

IN some countries large families were the rule,
While in others people, by taking precautions, avoided increase.

And there were those who had children for their own pleasure,
But who afterwards told them that they ought to be grateful.

‹ 19 ›

NUMBERS of people began to find no meaning in life,
And to ask each other what it was all about.

‹ 20 ›

SOME worshipped their bodies, while neglecting their minds;
Others worshipped their minds;
And their bodies, when exposed to view, looked all out of proportion.

Some made a god of sport, exercising their muscles and quickness of eye by every sort of game;
Others led lives so devoid of physical effort, that they took to doing health exercises in their bedrooms.

‹ 21 ›

MANY people lost faith in themselves;
And for those who felt unfitted for their tasks,
There were correspondence schools that advertised the sale of confidence and poise,
Which they declared to be the hallmarks of real prosperity.

‹ 22 ›

SOME spent their days in illness,
Cut off from work, from active life;
Passing the hours in silent contemplation wondering,
Being a burden, falling asleep.

Many were maimed in war.

‹ 23 ›

UNDER the action of injections and drugs, and as a result of
    improved sanitation,
The virulence of epidemics and minor illnesses constantly
    decreased;
While incurable diseases, cancer, madness, and suicide,
Became more common year by year.

‹ 24 ›

AND when men died their families were usually involved
    in complicated and expensive ceremonies;
While their places of burial were adorned with memorials,
Of a durable and costly nature.

‹ 25 ›

THE relationship between parents and offspring was often
    discordant.
Many people frightened their children by punishment, or
    cajoled them by appealing to their natural affection,

So robbing them of independence, and to some extent destroying their joy in life,
When their lives had hardly begun.

‹ 26 ›

In Europe, for the most part, man had no pleasure in worship,
And I never heard the sound of laughter in any church, chapel, synagogue or mosque.
In fact, it appeared that if a person did laugh in any of these places,
He would be put out.

The sects that included dancing and light music in their services,
Were regarded by western orthodoxy as being peculiarly depraved;
While the cult of the more amusing forms of ju-ju,
Was considered not to be worship at all.

‹ 27 ›

In the restaurants of the well-to-do there were unhealthy people, bejewelled and starched, glowing with the passing humour of good wine.
In the poorer eating-houses, there was frankness, friendliness and bad food.

‹ 28 ›

THE consumption of meat and alcohol, sugar and drugs, increased year by year.
In order to feed mankind, live cattle endured the sufferings of long journeys;
Their blood was often poisoned by unnatural feeding, or by the fear of death;
And in some countries sick animals were restored to apparent health by the injection of vaccines, before being taken to the slaughter-houses to be killed.
Frequently their corpses were frozen, and kept for long periods,
Before they were eaten.

‹ 29 ›

SOME men drank too much, while others did not drink enough.
And there were those who found in alcohol an escape from reality;
They caught, under its influence, blurred glimpses of happiness,
At the price of life made more elusive.
There were even minor poets and philosophers,
Who found in wine their only heaven.

‹ 30 ›

FOR the most part people ate and drank what they liked and could afford,

Without knowing what was healthy or necessary;
But there were those who were considered to be health cranks, because they were for ever discussing and taking thought about what they ought to eat;
Or because they wore unusual clothes.

Few there were among cultured Europeans, who had as true an instinct as the wild animals,
And who lived in dignity and perfect health.

‹ 31 ›

ON the faces of the inhabitants of many lands there was sadness;
And those races who lived in laughter, sunshine and laziness,
Were considered uncivilised.
Few there were among the nations, whose lives were made happy, and whose burdens were lessened,
By the inventions of modern science.

‹ 32 ›

MANY covered themselves with an excess of clothing—often inconvenient—as fashion might dictate;
And clothes sometimes marked distinctions between classes, races or sexes,
Or followed conventions for special occasions.

So that I saw men on hot days dressed in top hats, long black coats, starched collars and tight-fitting boots;
(I was told that they had business of importance)
And I observed that in one country, at state ceremonies, gentlemen of equal rank wore the same number of rings through their noses.
While in another land, ladies wore plumes of a uniform colour on their bottoms.
And at the court of a queen, gentlewomen who were being presented, all wore tufts of three ostrich feathers on their heads.

‹ 33 ›

Most people seemed afraid of sun and air;
And while the men and women of some tribes were ashamed to be seen naked,
Others unconcernedly grew fat, flabby or diseased under cover of their clothes.

‹ 34 ›

Houses were often ugly and over-embellished,
Frequently they were all of the same design, joined together in long rows, and placed alongside a traffic artery.
Sometimes the rich had more space than they required,
While the poor were crowded together.
And most people kept their houses locked.

It was not uncommon to see the work of men's hands
 exposed for sale in palaces,
While nearby men dwelt in slums.
This was believed to be an economic necessity.
And frequently men entombed the dead more sumptuously
 than the living.
This was believed to be an honourable custom.
But, on the whole, man was far more interested in live
 persons than in dead,
And mausoleums, even the most elaborate, were soon
 allowed to fall out of repair.

‹ 35 ›

SOME people burdened their houses with quantities of
 furniture,
Which they did not use;
Others preferred simplicity.
Not a few surrounded themselves with every new labour-
 saving device.
Yet others suffered inconvenience and hardship
For want of the bare necessities of life.

‹ 36 ›

IN places the countryside was neglected;
Large areas went out of cultivation; lands were denuded of
 forest;
And I saw streams, polluted by old tins and garbage,

Purified with chemicals;
And woods that were littered with paper.

⟨ 37 ⟩

THE numbers of police steadily increased;
In some countries they went armed with lethal weapons.
Crimes became more frequent.
A greater proportion of mankind spent time in prison.

⟨ 38 ⟩

SPORTS and games grew in importance.
The flying of long distances, and the climbing of high mountains
Thrilled the hearts of men.
While boxing and racing became matters of world-wide interest,
Very profitable to the promoters.

⟨ 39 ⟩

TRAVEL facilities improved every year,
And innumerable tourists journeyed about the world.

Every form of activity multiplied.
Great numbers of books were printed, journals and periodicals.
More and more laws were enacted;
Wealth grew.

The power held by man extended day by day;
The tension of life increased.

‹ 40 ›

NEWSPAPERS were for the most part biassed;
Their views were controlled by the interests which owned them,
And they were largely devoted to propaganda.
The less reputable were guilty of repressions, distortions and exaggerations;
Many recorded crimes and political events,
And truthful details of personal history.

‹ 41 ›

THERE were private detectives who advertised that they could find out things;
There were churches that declared that salvation could be had, and that people could escape punishment for their sins, by special arrangement with God;
There were doctors who said that they could put people right in no time, by using the latest vaccine;
There were men who said that they knew for a certainty which horse would win a race;
There were politicians who promised to make life sweeter if they were given power;
There were soldiers and sailors who said that they would protect men from danger, and that all might sleep safely in their beds;

And there were many people who believed in the private detectives, in the churches, in the doctors, and in tipsters, in politicians, and in soldiers and sailors;
And there were some who believed in the whole lot.

‹ 42 ›

IN temples there was mystery,
Veiled dimness—the long slow beat of drums;
An all-embracing symbolism.
In churches there were dark and perfumed ceremonies,
Services of heavenly beauty, blending the arts of ages;
Shadowy candle light; echoing peace;
Vestments, profound music and voices as of angels,
Held within a setting of the purest grace.
And there were hard things said in chapels,
About damnation and the world to come.
There was conversion with bands, unction in odd corners,
And flashes of brighter worship.

The splutterings and flickerings of an ancient flame,
Grown pale in death.

‹ 43 ›

THE theatres mostly presented the latest revues;
Lively modern music—song and dance;
Fantastic settings—gorgeous even,

And such a degree of nakedness as the law of each country allowed.
And there were serious clever plays ;
Some in which sex was still a matter of interest,
Some that dealt with problems,
Some that were funny.

‹ 44 ›
In the cinemas—wild dramas of the agile west,
Intermixed with Romance;
Plays that featured fops, dotted with overpowering close-ups of girls with soulful eyes—slopping tears,
Or of slitted brutes;
Great historical pageants,
Mighty conceptions of the future,
Comics that made people laugh,
Scientific films,
Travel pictures—bringing near far places of the earth,
Unrestrained creations—visions of a world unknown.

‹ 45 ›
But many governments believed that public taste was not to be trusted,
And film censors and play censors were appointed.
They smelt out political propaganda in works of art,
And in themes of sex they scented dirt.

‹ 46 ›

Dancing took strange forms:
Happy youths and maidens—moving, amidst dust and smoke, to the sound of a mechanical piano;
Well-dressed crowds—watching splendid ballets, in which they took no part;
Folk dances—revived by enthusiasts—long after they had lost their meaning;
Great ballroom dances—tuned by jazz;
Clever dances on a stage;
Village dances—to the sound of fearful music;
Erotic dances—planned for tourists—at a price;
Tribal people—dancing all night long until exhaustion came—loving their dances.

Yes, dancing took strange forms;
And there were those who said that it was the devil's work.

‹ 47 ›

In literature men delighted in reading of the realities of life,
The open voicing of the criticisms and doubts that flooded their own minds.
And there were books that found an echo in the hearts of men, because they portrayed the world of men's longings.

But both kinds got suppressed if they came too near to
　　truth.

‹ 48 ›
PUBLIC individuals took to publishing their diaries,
So that after they were dead, if not before,
People knew what they thought of each other.

‹ 49 ›
AND dilettanti gentlemen
Sat amidst art and
Burst
With joy,
Because they felt quite capable
Of writing modern verse.

‹ 50 ›
ART withered away or became largely divorced from
　　life.
Often it ran into forms that were meaningless to the
　　people;
And even those who were supposed to know
Made bad mistakes.
Many followed leaders and vogues;
Few were able to work sincerely.

Only in Japan art possessed the soul of men.

The masterpieces of past ages were crowded together into
    museums, where they were preserved and catalogued
    by experts.
Some people went there to worship the antique; others to
    acquire culture;
More still remained outside.

‹ 51 ›

Music became the worship or the scorn of the classics;
Or the scorn or the worship of the newest jazz—
Worship that often grew to love,
Scorn that sometimes turned to hate.
The meaning and sincerity of modern composition waned,
For commercialism and exploitation laid their hands upon
    it,
As upon all life.

But to many music was the solace of their days,
An escape from drab reality;
A vehicle which carried them out of themselves, into the
    land of truth;
That for a moment led them beyond the walls of
    identity,
To make communion with the rhythm of the worlds.

‹ 52 ›

Architecture gave a perfect impression of the blindness
    of life.

Railway stations looked like temples,
Churches like banks,
Houses like tombs or cakes or genteel abodes or insanitary slums.
But there were fine public buildings, and lovely country homes,
By way of contrast.

⟨ 53 ⟩

There were many critics;
Men who dissected and discovered the works of man,
Who patiently rescued beauty and worth from an avalanche of all that was considered second-rate;

And some who screamed abuse,
Who threw mud and innuendo at every phase of existence,
Dragging the origins of things out of a respectable obscurity,
Turning noble ceremony into childish farce,
Destroying men's confidence,
And making the loveliness and the grace of life
Seem a mockery and a slur.

There were others who taught discrimination, or who cultivated taste;
Who kept the élite from seeing or hearing whatever was not fit for them;

Who held a light to guide the uninitiated;
Or who made themselves into mirrors of truth.

‹ 54 ›

In the schools knowledge was usually suppressed or distorted—with the best of intentions,
For children were taught only whatever it was considered desirable for them to know.
Boys and girls, mostly educated separately, were lured by rewards, scared by the fear of punishment, or encouraged in healthy competition.
Their games, as well as their lessons, were often compulsory;
They were instructed more by word of mouth than by the practice of life;
They were endowed with a sound patriotism, and with a due sense of all that was fitting,
And above all, in some countries, with the means of making a living.

The maximum of work was obtained from children,
And it was attempted to fill them with the greatest possible amount of knowledge, without paying undue regard to their individual needs or capacities;
So that it was not unusual for youth, in whom nearly every creative impulse had been suppressed, to grow up to desire possessions and fame and power.

The majority of young people were glad when they left school,

The happiness they felt in freedom, and in the security of whatever employment awaited them,
Outweighed their doubts.

‹ 55 ›

THE masters and teachers were, for the most part, poorly paid;
Frequently their hands were tied by the rules and regulations of governing bodies;
Often they were too few in number to be able to carry out their work as they desired.
And both masters and parents commonly believed that the number of successes in examinations was more important than the happiness of children.

‹ 56 ›

CITIES and towns grew in size, and were overcrowded;
The land in them constantly increased in value;
Houses were constructed higher and higher;
And while some men built on open spaces and made profits,
Others gave plots for gardens and were regarded as public benefactors.

‹ 57 ›

TRAFFIC in the streets grew in speed and in volume to such an extent as to become a serious problem.

The numbers of people killed in road accidents increased
    year by year.

Public institutions multiplied,
Prisons, libraries, schools, hospitals, law courts;
Sanitation improved.

‹ 58 ›

THERE were masses of workers cultivating the fields and
    making things;
Masses of soldiers and sailors ready to fight for God and
    King and Country,
And for economic necessities;
Masses of policemen upholding the laws;
Masses of lawyers expounding the same.
The tension of life increased.

‹ 59 ›

PEOPLE felt the need to form societies—sometimes secret
    ones,
To wear strange robes,
To listen to speeches,
To propagate enthusiasms,
To have feasts and ceremonies,
Even to inflict cruelties upon their fellows,
Or to protect themselves, their children, or animals, from
    injury.

‹ 60 ›

THE youth of many countries banded together in quest of freedom and understanding,
To strive for a saner life.
Writers and thinkers put forth innumerable schemes,
Social panaceas of every kind;
New systems of economics,
New ways of gaining health,
New projects for entertainment,
New hopes of Heaven.

‹ 61 ›

THERE were political, social and religious movements;
And while faith in the older creeds lessened,
New beliefs and sects and teachers
Sprang up throughout the world.

There were anarchists and reactionaries,
Vegetarians and pacifists,
Sunbathers and lovers of nature,
Searchers after truth,
And those who communed with spirits.

‹ 62 ›

NATIONS maintained huge armies and navies,
Busy dockyards, military schools and grounds for manœuvres.

Western peoples trained primitive races to use modern weapons.
Armament firms devoted vast factories to the production of munitions.
And while some men gloried in war,
There were others, even professional soldiers who had spent their lives in fighting,
Who came at last to think war futile.

‹ 63 ›

THERE were sudden booms;
Land booms, gold rushes, races for concessions, share booms,
Scrambles where the greedy of gain tore to the scene;
Hordes of frantic men and women clawing, clutching, grabbing;
While parasites quietly gorged—
Until the slump came.

Then the parasites dropped off—glutted;
And the fleeced and ruined,
The disillusioned and the drained,
Those who had sacrificed solid means in hope of wealth,
Melted away—
Stung.

‹ 64 ›

INVENTION followed invention;
Every discovery of science that could be so used,
Was applied to the improvement of engines of war.

Submarines and aeroplanes, tanks and guns,
Were continually made more effective;
And arrangements were completed to asphyxiate the inhabitants of towns by gas bombs,
As soon as war broke out.

‹ 65 ›

UNDER the control of Trusts and Supermen,
Industry flourished.
To standardisation and mass production, was added the technique of scientific labour management.
Efficiency, economy and the elimination of waste,
Characterised every phase of manufacture and distribution.
New markets were organised;
Prosperity—measured by the volume of Trade and Profit—
Reached peak after peak.
Civilisation, propelled by the dynamism of mechanistic science,
Fired by the hope of gain,
Gathered speed.

‹ 66 ›

YET among the hills there were many quiet valleys;
The sound of running water; sunlight through the leaves;
Ferns and pebbles;
The patient, smiling earth.

THE EARTH 39

⟨ 67 ⟩

NATURAL wealth was acquired by individuals and companies—to be exploited for gain;
The treasures of the earth were poured out without thought for the future.
Energy, derived from natural sources, was made available in ever growing quantities.
Financial power increased, and was for the most part devoted to profitable uses.
Bitter were the struggles to obtain it.
Unemployment grew.
The tension of life increased.

⟨ 68 ⟩

SCIENCE diverged into specialism;
So that while one man might spend his days investigating the thorax of a beetle,
Another would pass his life in the study of some theory of electronic emission,
While a third surveyed the stars;
None realising that they sought the same thing.

⟨ 69 ⟩

PRACTITIONERS divided themselves into schools,
Each side gathered what authority it could,
And often regarded opponents as charlatans or fools.

< 70 >
IN some men the love of science, for its own sake, grew so strong,
That they were able to experiment on live animals without misgiving.
And there were psychologists who helped to steady the world, correcting the balance;
Re-educating those whose minds were twisted up ;
Releasing them to useful lives.

< 71 >
THE branches of different religions separated into sects,
Argued and fought and wrangled.

But I observed that even the poorer representatives of the Creator of the Universe
Had to pay their third class railway fares.
From which I concluded that man's business capacity
Was greater than his sense of humour.

< 72 >
TRADE was pursued as an object in itself, and for the amassing of riches;
Advertisement and propaganda extended in scope;
The sale of every sort of article was promoted;
Large profits were made.

Shops were stocked with vast quantities of goods;
Numberless factories and workers were employed in making them;
Food was adulterated and treated with preservatives—canned and bottled;
Large profits were made.

Speculation in stocks and shares increased;
In property, in merchandise and in raw materials;
Large profits were made—equal losses.

‹ 73 ›

STRIKE followed strike;
And the workers of the world were discontented.
The social conditions of labourers were often low;
They were crowded together in cities,
Or badly housed among the fields.

‹ 74 ›

EDUCATION had come to mean the acquiring of knowledge and of manners.
People found themselves holding professions and doing work
Which they disliked or felt to be useless.
Few were able to express themselves sincerely, in some creative art.

‹ 75 ›

MEANS of communication extended and multiplied,
Were faster and more certain.
Governments erected barriers to trade and movement,
Imposed tariffs and immigration restrictions.
The tension of life increased.

‹ 76 ›

THE rulers were often elderly;
Sometimes they became rich;
For the most part they were chosen from the supporters of
    parties or by heredity,
Without great regard to their personal qualities.

‹ 77 ›

POLITICAL organisations financed elections with money of
    uncertain origin,
But which was generally believed to have been subscribed
    by those who had interests to be served.
Waste, inefficiency and graft were not uncommon.
Suppressive measures and laws intended to better mankind
Were equally frequent.

‹ 78 ›

SOME countries were overcrowded, while other parts of the
    earth lay fallow for want of population;
And to some lands people were denied access, at the
    bidding of race prejudice, of vested interests or of fear.

‹ 79 ›

BRILLIANT Nordic gentlemen went out to rule the East.
Strong nations bullied or protected the weaker, or influenced them by financial means;
And the strongest mistrusted each other.

The motive of both individual and national acts,
Was very largely gain.

‹ 80 ›

THROUGHOUT the earth there was tension.
In the face of rapid changes and of unforeseen developments,
Professional politicians and diplomats were helpless;
And men grew frightened, hoping for a leader to arise.

‹ 81 ›

SUDDENLY would come war.
Rivalries were forgotten; party combined with party, nation with nation;
Classes sank their differences in the common cause;
Projects, that had been discussed interminably,
Were put in hand.

Comradeship and self-sacrifice—always underlying life—burst forth;
Money, energy, organising ability, production and destruction
Were poured out in quantities beyond belief.

Churches forgot their teaching and took sides;
Socialists forgot their socialism and joined the fight;
Men forgot their own interests, in the struggle to save civilisation and their fatherland.

Press, politicians, soldiers, priests—gave out unending propaganda;
Every expedient of crowd psychology was employed to fire the masses;
Every artifice was used to transmute the energy of men into bravery and brutality,
To encourage the public, instil venom and to fan the glow of enthusiasm.
Inventors worked day and night to produce new engines of destruction;
Profiteers amassed wealth;
Multitudes perished.
No degradation—no dishonesty—was too low to be employed in the struggle;
No abomination too unspeakable to be imputed to the enemy ;
No excuse too cynical to justify the utmost violence;
No sacrifice too great to be made.

Unthinkable, unmentionable cruelty fouled the slaughter;
Incredible heroism and devotion shone out in the hearts of men;
Stench and horror, fear and sordid ugliness,

THE EARTH

Killings, maimings, ghastly filth and noise,
Intermingled with beauty, fortitude and love.

A veil of concealment covered the earth;
Friends and enemies were bought by secret agreements,
Or by acts of grace;
Nations foundered.

‹ 82 ›

THEN, with victory, came the heaven of release;
Tears and laughter, blended in madness of joy;
The heartfelt thankfulness of a whole world;
And the solemn making of peace.

Promises were forgotten amidst the scramble for spoils;
And while idealism bargained with self-interest,
The beaten pleaded for fair treatment,
And experts calculated their capacity to pay.

Finally, the victors sometimes thought to exonerate each other,
And to forestall the judgment of history,
By making the vanquished acknowledge their guilt.

‹ 83 ›

THE scars of war soon healed;
Man's powers of production were so immense, that within a few months the shortage of merchandise was made up;

And within a few years the destruction was restored.
Trade rivalry recommenced, and the life of the earth resumed its accustomed ways,
With gathered speed.

‹ 84 ›

AFTER each war friendships and hatreds quickly dissolved,
So that the enemies of one fight became the allies of the next.
And if the victors sometimes considered each other with a deeper suspicion, on account of their added strength,
They as often showed a more active sympathy with the defeated,
On account of their greater weakness.

‹ 85 ›

AMONG the nations the uncertainty and the dissatisfaction increased;
Many forms of government were instituted and were overthrown;
Republican and communist, monarchies and dictatorships;
Making but little difference to the general life of the earth.

‹ 86 ›

INTERNATIONAL tribunals were set up;
Conferences for disarmament were held;
Each side struggling to safeguard its own interests;
So that the tension of life increased.

‹ 87 ›

INTO eastern countries the west brought modern roads and railways,
Irrigation and missionary zeal,
Security and justice, hospitals and sanitation.
Simultaneously new markets were opened, prosperity bestowed, and profits made.

And eastern philosophers came with their wisdom to Europe and America,
To be listened to with great respect.

In fact East and West tried to teach, and to learn from one another,
Their different ways of life;
And considered each others' civilisations inferior or superior—as the case might be.

‹ 88 ›

BUT the seeds of one civilisation, thrown into another,
Caused unexpected growths;
So that the East became in a ferment,
And the West began to question and to doubt;
While the South danced on.

‹ 89 ›

AND it seemed to men that scientific fact warred with religious belief;

That the ways of nature were eclipsed by the wonders of art;
While to many the poetry of machinery and the romance of commerce
Were hard necessities,
Divorced from the graciousness of life.

Philosophy and religion, science and art and industry
Were out of tune with each other,
And with the heart of man.

‹ 90 ›

As self-seeking came to be informed by suffering,
The tension of life increased.
On the one hand, interest opposed interest,
And war followed war, growing ever more terrible;
On the other, nations sought to form leagues of governments
And to make treaties of peace.

Race considered itself superior to race, people to people, class to class;
Presumption and humiliation, philanthropy and misery, desire and misunderstanding, industry and unemployment
Walked side by side.
Great was the struggle of man for himself.

⟨ 91 ⟩

THE tension increases,
So that in these days man's life is often an illusion and a disillusioning,
A promise of happiness, of adventure, and of usefulness,
Followed by inadequate fulfilment;
Wonder or boredom—uncertainty, drudgery, terror;
A snaring by comfort, or a struggle for existence;
A loss of liberty, and a stifling of creative impulse;
Disappointment, unbelief, ill-health;
An escape from reality in drink or drugs—in work, amusement, or religion;
Tyranny; introspection, and the giving of advice;
Respectability;
Divine rightness or divine resignation;
And release by death.

II

VISION OF THE EARTH

VISION OF THE EARTH

Darkness falls.
One by one great stars shine out—heralds;
Soon the multitudes of heaven,
To guide the night.

—I look out upon the Earth,
The sleeping, restless Earth.
Your history reaches here behind me—
Now to be closed.
There is a short watch left,
And then, the dawn.

I see a faint light in the East;
Red streamers cast around the sky,
Rose—gold—blue;
It is the Day.

The sun shines on my book;
O glorious Vision—
Paling my words to nothing;
O golden wisdom—
Lighting the Earth.

VISION OF THE EARTH

⟨ 1 ⟩

I SEE a new Earth;
An Earth that is alive—glowing with the care of man;
Man grown wise and free.

⟨ 2 ⟩

THE influence of different civilisations flows evenly around;
Races and nations and sexes understand each other,
Endue each other with life.

Invisible threads of sympathy cover the earth;
Science and religion, art and industry, are one in truth;
The motive of every act is love.

⟨ 3 ⟩

MEN accept men, and women accept women, and they
    accept each other,
At sight;
Because of the ways of them, because of the understanding
    in their hearts.

⟨ 4 ⟩

O WORK and love and laughter;
Happy, happy crowds;

Lights and colours;
Movement—beauty—joy.

‹ 5 ›

THE men of every land are at liberty to go where they will;
Trade is free;
The government of the earth is as one;
Peace reigns.

Vast spaces teem with industry;
The surface of the earth is positive and healthy,
Alive in conscious growth.

‹ 6 ›

IN men's work is freedom of expression,
In their faces is the calm of all experience,
In their eyes is friendliness and peace.

Their minds are for ever held in truth,
Their hearts are in accord with the purpose of the earth,
They know that they are equal,
Races and peoples, men and women.

They sing as they work,
They follow their desires,
They are in love with life.

‹ 7 ›

THE rulers are the wisest of men and women,
Those who have creative power and a sense of fitness;
So that life moves with all the delight and perfection
Of which man is capable.

‹ 8 ›

THE science of the earth is complete;
A wondrous pattern;
A parallelism and a crystallisation of all thought, into which
    every fact of life fits;
A growth that is projected in every dimension;
Rhythmical in movement,
Perfect in its infinite relations;
An indication of all knowledge—unbounded.

The sound of a phrase in the music of the worlds;
So clear as to amaze the mind of man;
So splendid as to dazzle his senses;
So beautiful as to fill his heart with unspeakable peace and
    joy.

‹ 9 ›

AND man,
Man and Woman,
The flower of the earth;
Certain and frank—strong and graceful;
With the look of gods—the handclasp of friends;

Having dignity and intuition;
Being clear and content ;
Radiating energy and love.

Masters of themselves—laughing and gay;
Changeable—happy—free.

⟨ 10 ⟩

THE Earth and its natural wealth;
The power that is derived from it,
Its favours and its fruit,
Are the heritage of man.
Inventions and discoveries,
Communications and financial power,
Are devoted to his use.

⟨ 11 ⟩

THE work that men do is vital to the earth ;
Done in gladness of heart,
A gift freely given ;
A creation from earth's materials—wrought by the strength and brains of those most fitted;
An ordering of earth's arrangements—guided by intelligence and humour;
An application of earth's science—devoted to the welfare of mankind;
A distribution of earth's bounty—
Made with love.

‹ 12 ›

THE towns are beautiful;
Centres of communication and exchange of thought and energy,
Of knowledge, merchandise and fun.
Happy towns,
Where art and entertainment are poured out, in ever varying forms;
Where truth is spread abroad.

‹ 13 ›

RULES are observed in understanding and content;
Only children, laughing, break them.
There is but one law,
The law of love.
Every thought of man is born in love;
Every deed is an act of love freely done;
And bodies are gifts of love and of passion,
Offered and accepted in gladness,
Conceived in laughter and delight.

‹ 14 ›

I HEAR music—
Clear, subtle, strong;
Ever changing, ever new, ever evolving in form;
Sounding out life's meaning and life's rhythm,
Wherein I lose myself.

‹ 15 ›

MARRIAGE :
Marriage is love;
Heart love, soul love, body love;
A state which all the world conspires to promote;
As common as the stars.

‹ 16 ›

MEN and women wear clothes that make glad the beauty of their bodies;
Varying with races, with seasons, and with individuals;
Suitable to the work in hand.

People go often naked in the open air, and in their houses.
It is the same to them as to be clothed.
Their bodies are handsome, sweet smelling, bronzed, glowing with health.
In their faces is contentment,
And their words are laughter and truth.

‹ 17 ›

ART is the eager growth of the earth.
Colours, forms and patterns—forged out of earth's substance;
Creations of love—made in joy and gusto;
Understood of the people,

In agreement with their life,
Spread throughout the world.

‹ 18 ›

DWELLINGS are lovely and agreeable—healthy and open.
Buildings grow into forms that express their meaning;
In keeping with their surroundings,
In relation to their materials,
Suitable to their use;
Strong—simple—fine.

‹ 19 ›

THERE are fêtes and carnivals, games and amusements;
What fun there is, and laughter.

‹ 20 ›

LIFE is a dance;
A movement of body and of mind in concert with the
 rhythm of the earth;
A feast in which all men take part;
The perfect expression of emotion.

Often at the changes of the seasons, in the evening, or at
 sunrise, or in a storm
People dance.
Dances grown out of the feeling of the hour,
Alloy of life and happiness and love,
Of power and of passion;

Keeping pace with the earth,
In tune with all her moods.

⟨ 21 ⟩

I PASS by furnaces and forges at night;
Lusty men smile at me through the glow and the sparks.
I see teams of builders, and constructors of bridges;
I meet companies of happy road-makers, and diggers of canals.

Their work is done in gladness,
And in their eyes is the light of the knowledge of use.
Everything that is made is beautiful and honest;
Everything that is done, is done with zest;
And all men go free.

⟨ 22 ⟩

THEY take me into strange places.
Here are companionship, lights, mystery;
The housing together of all the arts;
Colour, acting, songs;
Faithfully remembered tales;
New forms of life, tried out in counterpart,
Before they come to earth.

⟨ 23 ⟩

THE air is charged with voices, music, pictures;
The wonders of the earth, and of every part of the earth;

All history, past, present, future;
The secrets of every form and act of life.

Imagery in which time is accelerated, interrupted, or reversed;
Motion freed from laws;
Relativity drawn into the absolute;
Density compressed, or diffused;
Form distorted—dimensions multiplied.

Thus is the sequence of causation unfolded;
The perfection of growth—the rhythm of change;
Visions immense in time and space,
Infinite in movement;
Reflections of the progress of the worlds.

‹ 24 ›

THE fields and valleys, the forests and the hills,
Give forth abundance;
And all the countryside is kept in beauty.

‹ 25 ›

CHILDREN are surrounded by a world in being;
The outcome of every age and of every work of man, and of the earth;
By materials and tools, workshops and appliances;
Inventions and models, pictures and maps.

Everything that can be, is learnt by action and experience, from the use and the nature of things.
Boys and girls together; they are always busy, always happy, always free.

They build and make gardens, are carpenters and cooks;
They print and read, weave cloth and paint, and do all kinds of work.
Much of their life is passed camping in the open, playing in the sun, swimming and making journeys.

They create and control their own organisations;
They act and talk and sing and dance.

Every instruction and information that they seek, is accessible to them;
Every experience of the past;
Every practice of the present;
All that they can imagine of the future.

‹ 26 ›

AND when children leave school, they know the needs of the earth;
They are aware of their own capabilities and limitations, of their desires and dreams;
So that thereafter they are able to do the work they will,
With all their might.

‹ 27 ›

The means to all knowledge is within their reach;
Truth is awakened in their hearts;
They put forth creative energy in joy and happiness,
In love with all the world.

‹ 28 ›

Life is a triumph and a dance,
A love song and a harmony,
Born into the rhythm of the earth.

It dawns in sleepiness and wonder,
And the morning of it grows in freedom, to the need of doing things.
Romance outruns reality, while imagination strews the way with flowers—
Until youth comes of age.

Then opens into life,
Wisdom, and the happiness of work well done,
The joy of being a creator,
The grace of perfection,
The calm of fulfilment,
And all the pleasures of the earth—
Until the evening.

And in the dusk,
Man sets out again upon his road—
In peace.

III

LIFE

LIFE

I take into my hands the skeins of life.
Here threads are knotted and tangled and broken;
But in the maze of them,
I see a pattern.

Words and faces ; questions, theories, facts;
Actions and intentions; motives and results;
Contacts and dispersals;
Institutions, forms and growths;
All of life—intertwined.
And in the maze of it,
I see a pattern.

I do not weave;
Laughing, I tell the threads.
How could I weave ?
For I too am a thread,
Within the skeins of life.

LIFE

⟨ 1 ⟩

A FRIEND said :
Explain what you have written.
I answered :
My description of the earth as it is, is truth as I see it;
Observed and described as well as I am able;
Selected and arranged for the purpose of this book;
But neither distorted nor disguised.

The vision of the earth as it will be, is truth as I know it;
It lives in my heart, and one day it will live in the heart of the world.
That, to my knowledge, is certain.

⟨ 2 ⟩

THEN there came a number of people, saying:
We believe in the earth of your vision; what can we do to hasten the day of its coming?
I answered:
That day cannot be hastened by any external thing;
By any institution, or government, or system;
Its coming depends upon an awakening in the mind of man.

The only mind which you can awaken is your own;
And the way of that awakening is the way of life.

⟨ 3 ⟩

ONE asked me when the earth of my vision would come into being.
I answered:
In my heart it is already here;
And though I cannot know when it will awaken in the hearts of others;
Yet, the tension of life is so strong,
Uncertainty and suffering so widespread,
And the first notes of understanding so oft repeated,
That I feel the time is near.

⟨ 4 ⟩

I DO not care what happens.
I see the people of the earth, marching with certitude towards their goal.
I walk with them.
And if I have eyes to see a little further than the rest,
That will not make me sad.
Rather the contrary;
Knowing the happiness to come,
Adds to my delight.

⟨ 5 ⟩

BURIED deep in your heart is the knowledge of absolute truth and right.

LIFE

If, instead of putting your questions there,
You seek the guidance of philosophers, or religions, or great men;
Can you wonder that your heart should lose its faculty of speech?
And your mind its intuition?

⟨ 6 ⟩

A YOUNG man asked of me:
Say, how comes the difference between this world and that?
I answered:
In this earth man seeks for himself.
He goes after money or love or fame, power or ease;
Or he works for the joy of working, without knowing why.
In that, man does whatever he does, because he loves the earth;
Because he knows that he and all the people of the earth are one;
Because he loves every man as he loves himself,
In wisdom and in truth.

⟨ 7 ⟩

I TRAVELLED again over the earth.
I found the East seething with discontent;
And all Europe covered with war memorials,
Like pock marks after a disease.
I visited the dirtiest of industrial cities;

And the fairest gardens.
I walked through the glitter of the best-organised shops;
And wandered alone in the fields and over the hills.
I sat by streams and by the sea;
And my heart was filled with peace.

‹ 8 ›

Of the three main currents of life, I observed
Energy, from the West;
Wisdom, from the East;
Rhythm, from the South.
And all of these shall run together to inform life.

For energy without wisdom is blind;
Nor can they act effectively together,
Out of rhythm with the earth.

‹ 9 ›

I passed over a broad river,
Whose waters were red with the waste produce from some factory,
Whose surface was covered by a film of oil
In which no fish lived.

There are men who would so treat all the earth,
If they might gain.

⟨ 10 ⟩

THERE came into my mind a picture of the world as it might be,
And again the knowledge of the world as it is.
And I saw that the world that is,
Is a necessary stage in the evolution of the earth that is to come.

⟨ 11 ⟩

LIFE is a continuous adjustment to environment;
And only perfect intuition can bring perfect adjustment;
And when perfect intuition is attained,
Life becomes perfect happiness, without tension, capable of the complete response to every circumstance;
The free outpouring of creative energy;
Love, Nirvana, Paradise, Initiation; or whatever name conveys to you,
All that your heart desires.

⟨ 12 ⟩

ONE morning, as I started out alone,
A stranger saw me;
And straightway leaving his companions,
He came with me a while.
Then, calling me by my first name,
He gave me his good wishes.

I take them with me always.

‹ 13 ›

In the end, the earth does not tolerate domination;
Neither by races, nor nations, nor classes, nor institutions, nor individuals.
You can read that fact in history;
Or you can go on making more history,
And then read the same fact.
Nor does it matter that the dominating power consider itself to be the incarnation of rightness and benevolence.
It is a characteristic of dominating powers, to consider themselves incarnations of rightness and benevolence.

The period of each kind of domination varies with its nature;
Race domination being the longest,
Individual domination the shortest,
National, institutional, and class domination, lying in between.
But while domination lasts, it has a purpose;
A purpose which is outside its own knowledge.
And when that purpose is attained,
Domination ends.

‹ 14 ›

Do you think that these gentlemen, holding the balance in international politics, will hold it always?
Have you not observed that history is spotted with wars?

LIFE

And were not those wars waged, for the most part, in national interests?
Are not these gentlemen still speaking of national interests?
How then do you expect that there will be no more wars?
Do you imagine that a treaty or two, safeguarding national interests, will prevent them?

‹ 15 ›

IN a city I saw a full-grown man selling mechanical birds, that fluttered on the pavement;
Such was the work the earth gave to him to do.
In that same city were a hundred thousand clerks, passing their days in ill-lit offices;
Such was the work the earth gave to them to do.
Those mechanical birds, at least were in the sun.

‹ 16 ›

As I went into a great library,
I remembered that there is something more wonderful contained within one man,
Than in all the books on earth.

‹ 17 ›

A WOMAN asked me what kind of religion to adopt.
I said:
The kind that suits you best.
I tried every sort, before I found what I wanted;

And I found that, quite unexpectedly, within my own heart.
After which, I became a religion unto myself.

‹ 18 ›

AND to a man who enquired about philosophies,
I gave a similar reply.

‹ 19 ›

I CAME to a strange institute;
Where people in blue robes,
Sat in blue rooms,
Waiting for healing thoughts to come out of the distance;
Where I went.

‹ 20 ›

THE earth is like a human body.
And if one part of the earth seeks to direct all the rest,
It is as if one organ of the body sought to control the others;
It cannot be.
And if some nations try to isolate, or to ignore, another nation,
It is as if the organs of the body tried to dispense with one of their number;
In health, it cannot be.
But the whole shall work in harmony together.

‹ 21 ›

WHERE do you think we all are going?
I will tell you:
Towards happiness that is beyond dreams;
Towards truth that surpasses thought;
Towards realisation of something that is both within you
    and beyond you;
Towards freedom, peace and love.

‹ 22 ›

A MAN asked me:
What happens after death?
And I answered:
How should I know? You had better ask of a dead man;
Or better still, enquire of those spirits who return from
    beyond the beyond.
They at least talk.
Only remember that in all the history of the world, not
    one of them has yet made any communication,
Which matters to mankind.

‹ 23 ›

WITHIN this smoky city,
Dare you to build a house of God?
Dare you erect tall spires, that cannot pierce the mist?
Dare you sing praises, while all the sky is choked?

What is blasphemy?

‹ 24 ›
A MAN asked me if I knew of a lodging for the night.
While we searched together, we saw a multitude of motor-
    cars, furnishings, utensils, haberdashery;
All comfortably lodged for the night.

‹ 25 ›
I CAME to a fashionable ball.
In spite of many beautiful young people, of brilliant con-
    versation, lovely clothes, perfect taste, music, dancing;
In spite of silken walls, soft lighting, banquets, laughter;
In spite of all of these,
I saw unhappy faces.

‹ 26 ›
As I looked upon the world, I saw that everything that
    existed, both now and always, was necessary to its
    unfolding;
That no happening or condition was either good or bad;
That every act of man or of nation that grew out of har-
    mony with the earth, whether conscious or unconscious,
    would burn itself out;
To the end that man should enter into his heritage;
And be free.

‹ 27 ›
SOMEBODY spoke to me about the love of the body.
I answered:

LIFE

The body is the perfect expression of the soul.
If you love the body and neglect the soul;
Or if you love the soul and ignore the body;
You tear a sacred thing in two;
So causing pain.

⟨ 28 ⟩

I saw a bright shop, with coloured ribbons and ornaments.
Outside a lady gave a penny to a man,
And told him not to spend it on drink.

⟨ 29 ⟩

If you think there is anything that is wrong in this world,
    or that could be otherwise than it is;
It is you that are mistaken.
For the world, is a world growing up; and though you may
    be able to see a further stage of its growth,
You cannot make the intermediate steps less necessary.
Before birth there is travail.

⟨ 30 ⟩

There came an ardent communist, who said:
I will blow this casino to hell.
I answered:
Blow it.
I dare say someone will rebuild it,
Perhaps a trifle larger;

And if they catch you they may hang you,
Which will be good for you also.

‹ 31 ›

THERE came a sun-dried vegetarian, who said:
I will teach the world to eat herbs and the fruits of the earth.
I answered:
Teach it.
Some people will swear, and some will eat more fruit;
But in the teaching you will gain experience.

‹ 32 ›

I CAME to know that every act and every phase of life was, in its time and place,
Perfect;
And always had been perfect,
And always would be perfect,
In its time and place.
And I knew that the tension of the life of the earth,
Was the sign of man's awakening,
To peace and wisdom.

‹ 33 ›

To one in suffering, I said:

Have courage;
This is not for ever;

This is your crucifixion;
From it you shall arise to new life.

Have faith;
This is a barrier on your road;
And when you have crossed over it,
You shall know its measure and its need.

Take my hand;
For I have passed this way,
And know the truth.

‹ 34 ›

FOR ever emergence.
For ever the casting down of the old,
And the bursting forth of the new;
For ever, and for ever.

‹ 35 ›

I CAME to a pacifist meeting.
I said:
Peace is of the heart.
It cannot be maintained by political systems, by economics,
    or by diplomacy;
Nor by armament, or disarmament;
Nor by teaching the brotherhood of man;
Nor by any institution or treaty.

It is a free gift, which you may gather unto yourself,
But which you can bestow upon no man.

Peace is of the heart;
It is the child of love.

‹ 36 ›

A REASONABLE man said to me:
The world of your vision is not new;
It has been spoken and written of by many.
But it is a fallacy, the outcome of an unco-ordinated
    mind;
It cannot be proved to a person of ordinary intelligence;
It does not exist.

I gave no answer.

And one made enquiry of me saying:
Why did you not answer him?
Said I:
Every man believes what he finds in his own heart.

‹ 37 ›

THE way is the way of life.
If you are oppressed internally or externally;
By your thoughts or ambitions or hopes or fears or loves;
By your work or health or surroundings or employment or
    unemployment;

If you are unhappy or unbalanced or inert;
It is you that are out of harmony with life.
And it is only by getting into harmony with life,
That you can relieve the tension.

⟨ 38 ⟩

EVERYONE grows in his own way.
Some by supporting political systems,
Some by religion,
Some by science,
Some by social work,
Some by being vegetarians,
Some by industry,
Some by education,
Some by art;
And by many another road.

⟨ 39 ⟩

IF you scan the faces of people,
You may gauge the depths of their experience;
And your own face speaks volumes to them.

⟨ 40 ⟩

THERE is nothing to be condemned;
No social condition;
No institution;
No suffering.

All are inevitable and necessary in their place and time.
All are grown out of the life of the earth.
All will fall away, and cease to exist, when their use is passed.

Will you fight to bolster them up?
Will you hack away at their foundations?
It makes no difference.
The course of life is unaffected by your acts.
The only thing you can alter,
Is yourself.

‹ 41 ›

A REFORMER screamed at me:
Do you see nothing wrong with the earth?
I answered:
Does a bird see anything wrong with an egg?
Assuredly neither earth nor egg have completed their
    growth;
But the world evolves unceasingly.
Every hour, every day, every month, brings changes.
It is hard to imagine the life of a century ago;
That of ten thousand years past is forgotten.
Yet surely it was right for its period.
So also the life of the earth of to-day is right for to-day.
And the life of the earth of to-day, as of all times,
Includes all works and professions, not excepting reformers.
No; I see nothing wrong with the earth;
And nothing wrong with you.

‹ 42 ›

You cannot get peace by believing you have it;
Though you may find consolation.
You cannot get rest by taking care;
Though you may postpone discomfort.
You will not find love in a bottle of wine;
But many a pleasing illusion.

‹ 43 ›

A GIRL came to me saying that she sought a friend.
I told her, that such friendships as were for her, would come her way without much seeking;
And that, that perfect love which she desired, was very near to her;
Only that its image was clouded by her own feelings,
So that she could not see it,
Nor it, her.

For love is as hard to receive as it is to give;
And can only be given perfectly,
By the free in heart.

‹ 44 ›

I WENT down a coal mine.
Through the darkness;
Through the damp and treacherous atmosphere,
I watched;

Watched men working,
Working for wages that a retailer of scented soap would consider as beneath contempt.
From his point of view,
He would be right.

‹ 45 ›

THERE came a young man who sneered at most of the activities in the town;
At the antique dealers, the jewellers, the stamp collectors, the sellers of faked-up food and of drugs.
I said:
So does the world grow up.
Have you forgotten your own past?

‹ 46 ›

MY road was barred by a procession of young people.
Hundreds, thousands passed by;
Singing, shouting, waving red flags.

Comrades, what are you seeking?
International peace?
That is true.
The brotherhood of man?
That is true also; not only of the proletariat, but of all men.
Freedom?
That too is true;

As true, as certain, as the earth and the stars.
Who in all the world is more sure of that than I?

Yet—you will find none of these things in the road in which you are.
Do not misunderstand me.
It is not wrong to sing and wave red flags;
It is not wrong to struggle and to search;
You will not cease from searching until you find that which you need.
None of these things are wrong.
But political or economic changes will not bring you to your goal.

When you find that you are on a false road, and all seems dark,
Keep on singing;
Here is a map.

‹ 47 ›

ONE day as I swam in the pool of a spring,
A party of tourists—male and female—came to inspect that place.
They did not know that I was naked,
Until I climbed out.
Then they fled, with cries and twitterings;
Like a lot of doves disturbed by a snake.

Yet we were of the same race;
And I meant them no harm.

‹ 48 ›

If you think that a high priest in his robes, saying meaningless nothings, is any more ugly or less beautiful than a swearing navvy; you do not see clearly, nor hear aright.
Each is as necessary as the other;
Both are essential to the evolution of the earth;
And clearness of vision shall come to you,
At about the same time as it comes to them.

‹ 49 ›

I came to a company of artists.
I said:
These dreams that fill your lives,
That struggle for expression,
Are the reflection of something which is beyond you, yet very near to you;
Something which very few of you have ever reached;
Something which one day you will all see and touch and hold.
What greater promise can I make to you than that?

‹ 50 ›

Some diplomats said to me:
Your words threaten our sacred national rights.

I answered:
In the future, your sacred national rights will dissolve into nothing.
My words do not affect the matter.
The songs of birds neither hasten nor delay the spring.
Like them, I make an announcement;
And I enjoy myself.

⟨ 51 ⟩

I MET a man who was trying to give a whole race the chewing-gum habit.
He made use of every invention that science produced;
Of the printing press, electric signs, cinemas, radio, aeroplanes.
He told me that his advertising was the most efficient on earth.
He said that no one could teach people the value of chewing-gum quicker than he could.
He mentioned the amounts of chewing-gum per head per year that each town in his area bought.
And he showed me figures of the quantities which each town might be expected to buy,
When he had given them the chewing-gum habit.

He said that there was money in it.

⟨ 52 ⟩

AND I knew a travel agency that boomed Egypt.
So that people from all over the world,

Who wanted to go somewhere,
Went to Egypt.

‹ 53 ›

Above—I saw the stars.
Below—the light in a window.

‹ 54 ›

I came to the house of a whore.
Long, long, we talked of life, happiness, and love;
For these things, she said she had missed,
And had money enough for that day.

‹ 55 ›

I came to the house of a lady.
We talked of ourselves, of books, theatres, politics, and of
    the doings of our friends;
For she could not speak of all that she had missed,
But had money enough for her life.

‹ 56 ›

I came to the hut of an African.
And he, with his friends, danced far into the night;
So glad they were to see me.

‹ 57 ›

There is not anything on earth that has more meaning, or
    importance, than you ;

No building, no work of art, no machine, no institution, no organisation.
There is no person on this earth who is not your equal, and of whom you are not the equal;
And it does not matter if you are old or diseased or poor or helpless or rich or famous;
And if you think that you are superior to any man, or that any man is finally superior to you, you live in illusion.
Everything that any man, or any collection of men, usurp from others, will be restored in the end.
Any man that thinks himself better than another, that is shocked by another, by another's colour or clothes or habits, is not at ease with life.

‹ 58 ›

ALL life is a great design;
Every part of it dependent on the other parts;
Interlocked, intertwined,
Moving in perfect harmony;
Free in action and inevitable in reaction.

‹ 59 ›

A WOMAN asked me:
You have said that all men are equal; what do you mean by equal ?
I answered:
I do not mean equal in mind or in body ;
For some men have strong bodies, made for labour;

While others have fine intellects, capable of science.
And this will always be so;
Since the earth has need of workers both with hands and with brains.

But every man, and every woman, is equal in the sense that they all contain within themselves an essence of the source of the life of the whole universe.
So that their origin is the same,
And one could not exist without the other existing;
And each is equally necessary to life.

Some day man shall discover this;
And then, he shall care for the miner, equally with the artist;
For scientists, equally with the women of the fields.
And he shall know that races and nations and sexes,
Have each an equal heritage,
And an equal meaning.

‹ 60 ›

A SEEKER came saying:
I have searched the modern philosophers for a confirmation of your words.
I answered:
The spirit of life lives in no philosophy;
It lives in no religion, in no system, in no institution, in no school.

It lives in life.
And it can be met with, in yourself.

‹ 61 ›

By accident I came into a place where a lot of old men and women were discussing truth.
What I heard there filled me with utter amazement;
And with unutterable joy.

‹ 62 ›

Can you face your own body, and accept every part of it, and all its acts?
Can you face your own mind, and understand and accept every thought it has,
And has ever had?

‹ 63 ›

A man said:
I have been cheated.
I answered:
Is it so?
Has the cow cheated the grass?
Or the trees the earth?
Each of us shall receive, and use, and restore:
Our learning to science;
Our love to our friends;
Our possessions to men;
Our bodies to the earth.

Poor use, or sudden loss,
Feel like being cheated.
But the earth is lavish of her gifts.

‹ 64 ›

Without illness there could be no hope of health;
Without war there could be no hope of peace;
So, without death, there would be no hope of life.

‹ 65 ›

There came a soldier fresh from making history, saying:
You have rated me with the cultivators of the fields.
I answered:
I have assessed no values.
Every man performs his work in accordance with his lights.
But the world has rated you as a maker of history;
And the world has not yet observed that the cultivators of
    the fields,
Are also making history.

‹ 66 ›

Fear not.
If you see the whole world going to war;
Using every instrument of death that science can devise;
Fear not.

If cities get gassed out; and you watch the choking remnants
    dying in the fields;
Fear not.

If you find yourself a judge, passing futile sentences upon
   those who cannot help themselves;
Fear not.

Or a worker making useless things;
Fear not:
Nor curse.

For all things that exist are the needs of life, and of life's
   fulfilment.
The issue is not in doubt.
Even though darkness cover the world,
The sun returns.
The times of the earth neither hasten nor delay.

‹ 67 ›

A POLITICIAN asked me:
What is the best form of government for this place?
I answered:
Whatever form exists.
He said:
But should not men desire to change their government?
I answered:
They will change it, and it will change, as they
   change.
If it goes too fast for them, they will pull it back.
If it moves too slowly, they will hasten its proceedings.

‹ 68 ›

A MAN said to me:
All my life is destroyed by unhappiness; I can find no meaning in it.
Why am I alive?
Why do I work?
What good is it?
What is it for?
What does it mean?
Why cannot I have what I want?
I said:
All this book is intended as an answer to your questions.

‹ 69 ›

THERE will come a day when people of all races shall be free to grow up into every type; to develop their individualities to the full;
When the conventions and customs that fetter mankind shall be no more;
When men's feeling for life shall be so true that they will live in harmony with their surroundings;
When infinite variety shall be the rule.

‹ 70 ›

I MAKE no complaint.
This is a perfectly good earth.
I, for one, cannot improve it;
And do not want to.

‹ 71 ›

You need have no doubt about the energy and the power of mankind.
When you consider the cities that have sprung up through the centuries, and in particular in the last hundred years;
The railways, steamships, factories, roads, canals, buildings, motors, aeroplanes;
The tremendous output of machinery, merchandise, pictures, books, music;
The extent of agriculture:
You need have no fear that mankind is likely to perish from inertia.

‹ 72 ›

EVERYTHING that you see in life, you see in the mirror of your own mind.
And if your mind be warped or cloudy, so shall the image of what you see, be warped or cloudy.
But when your mind is clear, life shall appear to you,
Clear and beautiful.

‹ 73 ›

I CAME across parents who taught their children to display a respect they did not feel;
To pretend a belief in what they did not understand;
To appear happy when their hearts were sad;
To act lies.

‹ 74 ›

I MET some people who lived among the debris of the past;
Who had old titles and old houses;
Who came out at intervals to bask in the public sunshine;
Like lizards.

‹ 75 ›

I CANNOT argue.
I tell of life as I see it.
But I do not see it through your eyes;
Nor can you look through mine.

‹ 76 ›

I AM a part of the earth.
If this book of mine be out of harmony with life,
It will die of itself.
If it accord with the rhythm of growth,
It will live and multiply,
And become absorbed into life—losing identity.
I could not regret it any more than a seed regrets the tree it has put forth;
Nor delight in it less than the earth delights in fallen leaves

‹ 77 ›

A MAN asked me to join a society for the prevention of evil;
Another—for the promotion of good;
One—for the education of the young;

Yet another—for the care of the old.
I thought:
I already belong to a society that includes them all.

‹ 78 ›

THERE came to me a priest.
All my life, he said, has been spent in the service of God;
and with all my heart I believe.
Yet, in your writing, I have found no word of Him, nor
of prayer, nor of worship.   Nought of the Churches.
I answered:
So long as you of the Churches have faith;
So long as even a few shall gather together to receive a
message of hope and salvation at your hands;
So long shall you minister to them.

But in the end, they shall be few indeed;
And your faith, and theirs, shall emerge into that know‑
ledge which is the Peace of God.
Then shall your forms of worship melt, as the snow melts;
To give light to that which it protects.

Your work has not been in vain.

‹ 79 ›

THERE came a young man, who said:
I have visited many schools and colonies and youth camps,
but I have not found in them that for which I sought.

Often there were people who were far from life ; faddists,
    fanatics, whose very appearance and clothes seemed a
    barrier between them and mankind,
And who lacked balance.
I answered:
Yet in them was the urge to find truth.
For every man his own road.

‹ 80 ›

YOUR greatest aid is the nearest thing to you;
Your best road is the road you are on.
If any man tell you that he has the only truth, the only
    religion, the only way ;
He deludes himself ;
And he may delude you.

‹ 81 ›

A WOMAN spoke to me of prisons.
I answered:
So long as a body secretes poison,
So long will that body strive to find means to protect itself
    from the poison which it breeds.
While society continues to manufacture criminals,
Society will continue to provide prisons in which to house
    them.
But a time will come when crime and prisons will be un,
    known.

‹ 82 ›

I ARRIVED at a conference for the propagation of forgotten tongues.
I said:
Gentlemen—the words of these dead peoples,
Do not amount to man speaking to man.
A day will come when every race shall talk the same language.
You cannot hold back the years.

‹ 83 ›

A MAN asked me if I could assist him into the Kingdom of Heaven.
I answered:
Neither I, nor anyone else; not in the sense you mean.
It is as if a caterpillar had asked to be helped to become a butterfly.
The fact is that, when its time is fulfilled, the caterpillar will become a butterfly.
And that time cannot usefully be shortened or increased.
Any attempt at external interference, is likely to end in harm.

It is the same with you; and my assistance is neither necessary nor desirable.

Only one thing:
It seems clear that the more healthy the caterpillar in body and mind,

The finer and more perfect will be the butterfly;
And if anyone can help in this matter,
It is the caterpillar itself.

Since you are the caterpillar in question,
These considerations may be of interest to you.

⟨ 84 ⟩

There came a joiner.
He said:
I work fitting palaces in ships;
Wondrous dining rooms, and saloons,
And magnificent private suites.
But with every work of my hands I leave a curse for the fools who enjoy these things.
For I, and my wife, live in a wretched one-room tenement; no light and little air.
We have no child.
We wouldn't be so cruel as to bring a child into that.
And I devote my spare time to sowing discontent among my comrades.

⟨ 85 ⟩

A woman asked me:
What is sin?
I answered:
Men set up arbitrary standards of right and wrong,

LIFE

Standards which vary with peoples, times, and places.
Sin, or crime, is the measure of the difference between acts and standards, at the time and place to which they refer.
Thus: among one people it is a crime to sell alcohol;
Among another people, it is not.
In one place it is a sin to go unclothed;
In others, nakedness is encouraged.
In peace time it is a crime to kill a man;
In war time—a crime not to.
What one age regards as highly amusing and desirable,
Another considers gross indecency.

Sin and crime are not, in fact, fixed conventions;
But change to suit the variations of human needs.

‹ 86 ›

I DO not sit in judgement.
For I discern nothing as between judges and criminals;
Between evil and good.
All to me are faultless in their place;
And one is not greater, nor less, than the other.

‹ 87 ›

ONE asked me:
Why cannot I see what is so clear to you?
I answered:
The flowers cannot bloom before their season;

Nor the sun rise before the dawn.
Have patience therefore, and remember a promise I have made.

⟨ 88 ⟩

A MAN from the Far East said to me:
We do not believe in the freedom of growth.
Man is neutral in character, neither good nor bad;
It is only by the highest moral teaching that he attains to perfection.
I answered:
By so thinking you confuse the spirit of life with some external thing; to be imprisoned in the mind, or imposed upon it.
To you it is as if a child were an empty vessel, into which to pour perfection, to make a perfect man.
But a child is the product of universal energy; able to evolve of itself; growing up into life.
If therefore you allow children to form into perfect vessels; strong, beautiful, happy, healthy; in harmony with life;
There shall freely grow within them, a part of the spirit of all things; which is, in itself, perfection and truth.
But if you seek to mould and to form children,
You will but succeed in warping the vessel which life has made for itself;
And so restrict life's growth.

‹ 89 ›
ANY man that sets his faith in any institution or system,
Has not awakened the faith that is in him.
Any man who does not wholly accept the earth, and all the people on it, and his own body,
Is in chains.

‹ 90 ›
WHATEVER you do, is work for the earth.
Its usefulness depends upon your wisdom;
Its measure upon the energy which you expend;
And its effect shall be in relation to your sympathy,
With the rhythm of life.

‹ 91 ›
A LADY spoke to me of schools for her son.
I told her:
There is every kind of school.
There are the great orthodox schools, which keep close to my description of schools as they are.
And there are some, a few, which draw near to the likeness of the schools of the future.
In between, there is every different shade;
The number of each kind, corresponding to the needs of the day.
Perhaps you will choose whichever you prefer;
Perhaps, the one your son prefers.

‹ 92 ›

People came to me saying:
This is fatalism, and that materialism—here are romanticism, classicism, socialism; and so forth.
I answered:
To you it may be so; but to me it is as if you were classifying water, saying:
Here is an eddy, there a whirlpool—here calm, there turbulence.
Yet even while you speak, the breaking waves turn to smoothness;
And under still waters, hidden currents flow.
Life is not a static thing;
But perpetual, dynamic change.

‹ 93 ›

If you think you will find what you are seeking in this book, or in any other book,
You are mistaken.
You will find it in yourself.

Here, there is nothing for those that find nothing;
There is nothing that will convince those who want to be convinced;
Nor those who do not want to be convinced.

But there is a message for anyone that can receive it.

‹ 94 ›

THE stream of life flows ceaselessly on.
If at one moment the waters seem to you tormented and broken,
Yet there are smooth and gentle reaches further down;
And not the smallest drop of that river,
Can flow out into the sea of understanding,
Without passing by the place of anguish.

‹ 95 ›

ON my journey, I came to a third class waiting room,
Where the latrine was so filthy, that I would not use it.

On my way out to the fields,
I passed a mason carving grave stones;
A church, kept spick and span;
A war memorial, gay with flowers.

So do men delight to honour the dead,
While neglecting the needs of the living.

‹ 96 ›

CAN you bring your mind into tune with all earth's moods?
Can you learn to accept the nights as well as the days?
    Winds and storms and fogs, as well as sunshine and fair weather?
Can you feel at home in the country and in towns? In factories and markets and exchanges?

Can you awaken in yourself the desire to consciously fulfil earth's purpose, letting your own motives die?
Can you open your heart to the knowledge of what earth's purpose is?
Can you refuse to accept anything from anybody that contradicts your own experience?
Can you learn the freedom of the mind?

⟨ 97 ⟩

I AM sufficient for myself.
There is nothing in this world I am afraid of.
There is nothing that I need;
Nothing which I do not really possess;
Nothing which I am not master of;
Nothing which I do not understand.
I am free.
I love life.
All experience is my friend;
And I am utterly content.

Thus sings my soul.
And if sometimes her words sound faint to me,
Shall I not write them down while they are clear?

⟨ 98 ⟩

A MAN said to me:
You tell me that there lies within me the possibility, nay the certainty, of an awakening in which I shall know the meaning of life, and attain to peace and happiness.

Can you prove this to me?
I answered:
I cannot.
If I could, the earth would have no need to exist.
For it is the object of the life of the earth, that man should come to that consciousness of which you speak.
Its coming shall be like the dawn of self-consciousness, which, having come, is itself the most certain fact of existence;
And which, to men, since they have it, needs no proof;
But which cannot be communicated to the animals, who have it not;
Far less can it be proved to them.
There is no means, no language, by which such a communication could be made:
No basis upon which any proof could be established.

And yet, I am myself the proof of every word that I have written.

‹ 99 ›
THE flow of life cannot be stopped,
Neither as a whole, nor in its parts.
It shall continue for ever, throwing up new forms, new institutions, new experiences.
And every form and phase shall be discarded, so soon as it becomes outworn, and of no further use;
Both in life as a whole, and in individuals.

‹ 100 ›

CHINESE moral law, American progress, French civilisation, Indian thought, Japanese culture, German organisation, Russian political systems, British empire, African rhythm;
Are all to be absorbed in the end.
It is inevitable; it is their purpose.
They shall all contribute to that life of the earth which is to be liberated in the heart of man.
Every institution created by man shall contribute to it.
Every work of man shall contribute to it.
Every thought of man shall contribute to it.

‹ 101 ›

I PROMISE you love.
I promise you that sometime you shall meet and hold and be held by, a lover;
A lover in whom shall live every ideal of your imagining;
Whose body shall be as beautiful to you as the sky;
Whose movements, and whose actions, shall mean as much to you as your own life;
Whose mind and whose soul and whose being, shall be as near to you as truth;
To be with you for ever.

‹ 102 ›

I CAME to an old garden of Japan.
Such loveliness and peace took possession of my heart

That I would have stayed there always;
Had it not been that I sought for something else.

‹ 103 ›

THE day will come when one man will no longer be considered superior to another on account of the colour of his skin,
The nature of his work,
The names of his ancestors,
The extent of his knowledge,
The amount of his wealth,
The number of his accomplishments,
Or the strength of his muscles.

‹ 104 ›

ONE came and said:
Be our leader.
I answered:
That cannot be; for there are as many roads as there are people,
And you alone can walk your own.
No religion, no political system, no personal leadership,
Can finally bring you to your goal.

‹ 105 ›

A MAN said to me:
You have not been fair to many existing institutions;
To schools, or religions, or national aspirations.

I answered:
I have only remarked on those characteristics of things
    which are the most certain to change;
And I have stated that, to my knowledge, everything that
    is, is perfect in its time and place.
Further I know that what was fitting for yesterday,
Will not be fitting for to-morrow.
And fairness and fitness are aspects of the same
    thing;
They are aspects of truth.

< 106 >

EARLY one morning I came to a field hospital.
In one ward there were twelve beds, neat and empty.
That night, the sister told me, twelve men, young men and
    strong,
Had left their mutilated bodies there.
That day, she said, she would write out ten messages,
Ten farewell messages; to friends and lovers.
(The other two had died unconscious.)

While I waited, the beds began to be filled again,
With the debris of that night's battle;
And I went out alone.

There was something in her eyes that made me think her
    mind might become disconnected from herself;
In mercy, leaving her insane.

‹ 107 ›

ALL night long I heard a man screaming.
Screaming because his arms had been torn off, and his body pitted by a hundred pieces of granite, thrown up from a shell-burst.

All night long I heard a woman sobbing;
Because love had brought her a child,
And her neighbours mocked her.

All day long I saw the sad face of a boy.
Sad because his parents did not understand him;
Because they petted him and punished him;
Because they guided him and moulded him and taught him.

All day long I heard some children playing;
And building and shouting and dancing and crying and laughing.

Signs and tokens.

‹ 108 ›

I CAME to a meeting of Scientists, Politicians and Financiers.
They cited statistics of the present, and considered proposals for the future;
They agreed to increase facilities, and so achieve greater results;

They determined to hasten progress, and to swell production;
To spread civilisation, and to advance prosperity.

It was as if they thought that volume and speed were the chief attributes of a heavenly life;
And that the acquisition of knowledge, accomplishments, riches and modern improvements,
Were the objects of existence.

In all their statistics I found but little mention of health;
And none at all of happiness or love.

But their energy was wonderful.

‹ 109 ›

Many came asking for particular advice.
I answered:
There is no advice of a personal nature that I can give.
For the actions of each one of you depend on your own reactions to what is, in a sense, outside you.
And I am one of those that are in your environment.
In my words, and in the words of others, you shall find what is suitable to you.
But if you would know what to do, in the circumstances in which you are,
Search your own heart.

⟨ 110 ⟩

A MAN asked me to explain the contradictions of science.
I answered:
Science progresses along two roads:
Firstly towards causes, towards simplicity, unity and truth.
Secondly towards effects; an ever-dividing specialisation,
    leading to systems and growths of endless beauty.
But this second road leads also from beauty to simplicity,
    to unity and truth.
So that the opposing directions are like the two halves of
    the same circle,
Meeting again.

Further;
Religion and industry, arts and institutions,
Are all phases of the science of life.
And what is true of science,
Is also true of them.

⟨ 111 ⟩

A MAN asked me:
What political system shall I support?
I answered:
The one in which you have most faith.
But remember that systems cannot in themselves change
    the heart of life.
And in so far as any system is based on profit or on domina-
    tion,

It will be upset.
And in so far as it is based on love and freedom,
It will live.

‹ 112 ›

THE structure of our society is founded on gain.
If you could alter the structure, without changing the
    motive underlying it,
You would produce an unbalanced thing;
Which, whether it fell or not, would rebuild itself in its
    own likeness.

Therefore, if you would work in permanence,
Strive to change the motive of life.
And the only part of that motive which is in your keeping,
Is your own.
You can change that ; but you cannot change mine,
Or anyone else's.

‹ 113 ›

Do you love your body ?
It is well.
But if it seems to you that by stuffing it with impurity, you
    worship it,
You have yet a long way to travel.

Therefore, when you meet a gross man, with a paunch,
    and flabby;

Or a painted lady;
You may well ponder in love and insight upon their ways.

And when you meet a fine man, full of years and beauty,
Wondrous in health and carriage and looks,
You may well rejoice.

⟨ 114 ⟩

THERE came a number of bankers, and successful burglars, and profiteers; together with others who had gathered up a fair share of this world's goods.
They said:
You have written that our profits are harmful to the earth.
I answered:
I have written nothing of the kind.
Your great collections are the necessary products of the life of our time; and are, in themselves, excellent.
But there will come a day when man's life will be no longer based on fear, and on the need to hoard.
Then such accumulations will be out of place;
They will not, in fact, exist.

⟨ 115 ⟩

FACES of children;
Happy, laughing faces,
To grow to perfect men.

Give them the teaching that you give;
Give them the life that you lead;
And then,
Look at the faces of the old.

Sorry, discontented faces;
Disillusioned, tired faces;
Anxious faces;
Sick.

But sometimes,
A noble aged face;
To declare to you a promise of the future;
And to call to mind,
Faces of children.

⟨ 116 ⟩

I AM not offering you anything.
I am not offering you salvation.
I am only telling you, that if you want it, you will have salvation, enlightenment, initiation, cosmic consciousness, peace;
Call it what you will.
It is inevitable.
Nothing can alter that fact.

⟨ 117 ⟩

THERE came a young woman, who said:
I love a youth. Often we sleep together.

I feel in my heart that this is right;
Yet my parents, and relations, and the priest,
Would think it wrong.

I answered:
Right and wrong are relative things.
If your ways are in accord with earth's purpose,
They shall live in the light of your own happiness.
But if they run counter to the earth,
They shall be guided by suffering,
Until you are again in harmony with life.

〈 118 〉

I say what I have to say, and whether you like it or not, makes no difference to me;
Nor to you;
Nor to anyone else.
But you will accept it in the end.

〈 119 〉

There came many who asked me:
What work shall we do?
I answered:
The work that is in front of you.
And they objected, saying that their work was useless, or underpaid.
I answered: How so?

The work of the earth is necessary to the growth of the earth;
And when any phase of it shall be no longer necessary, it shall cease.
Is it useless for leaves to put forth in spring, because they shall fall in winter?
Is the life of a caterpillar of no avail, because it shall become a butterfly?
If you suffer, it is on account of your own growth;
And when the growth that caused your suffering has been attained,
That suffering shall be removed.

⟨ 120 ⟩

In these days, when there are awakening in men's minds thoughts of the world that is to be,
What more common cause of impatience, than the picture of the world that is?
But the earth that is, is necessary to the earth that is to be;
Out of which it shall indeed grow;
And the earth is patient.

⟨ 121 ⟩

A man asked me:
Can you teach me the Truth?
I answered:
I cannot.
The Truth is.

You see it, or you do not.
Or you see one aspect of it; or another.
I can tell you what I see, as well as language will permit me.
That is all.
I cannot see for you.

⟨ 122 ⟩

Stock-brokers and property owners,
What are you getting excited about?
I tell you that share-scrip and title-deeds shall become meaningless things.

Soldiers and politicians,
What are you getting excited about?
I tell you that every empire shall fade out of existence.

The earth shall exchange all these for something immeasurably greater.
Meanwhile you do work that has to be done.
So what am I getting excited about?

⟨ 123 ⟩

I am part of the earth,
And I know it.
And everything that I do, I do for the earth,
Even as I now write.
And whatever the earth does to me, or to my work,

Is the same to me;
For I and the earth are one.

‹ 124 ›

For seven years I stayed in India.
If there be anywhere on earth, where wisdom is enshrined
    in the heart of man,
Surely it is here.

‹ 125 ›

If you become a slave of the mind, and neglect the body,
Or if you become a slave of the body, and neglect the mind,
You are unbalanced.

The needs of the mind are: creation, interest, knowledge,
    thought, repose and love.
The needs of the body are: sex, food, cleanliness, warmth,
    rest and work.
If you can accord all these to the rhythms of life,
You will have happiness and health.

‹ 126 ›

Do you think that there is anything more perfect than this
    earth?
I tell you there is not.
Do you think that there is anything that exists on this
    earth that is not perfect?
I tell you there is not.

LIFE

The seed is perfect;
The seedling perfect;
The plant perfect;
The bud perfect;
The flower perfect;
The fruit perfect;
And the seeds of the fruit perfect;
And so on for ever.

But the perfect seed is not the perfect fruit;
Each in its turn grows out of the other.
Flowers and trees; temples, brothels, factories and schools;
    men and women;
All are the perfect expression of themselves.
And these perfections are relative in time;
And as time passes,
Their expression changes.

The world that is to,day, grew out of the world of yester,
    day;
And the earth of to,morrow, is forming in the earth of
    to,day.
And you, and I,
Belong to the world of to,day;
Having come from yesterday;
With a journey to make, into to,morrow.

That is why we sometimes find it uncomfortable,
Stopping where we are.

‹ 127 ›

ONE objected, saying:
If there is nothing wrong with the earth, it is not necessary to do anything.
I answered:
You cannot stand still.
Growth, the expenditure of energy, is the very cause of your existence.
Every day, every hour, you are forced to act;
And will be forced, until you die.
Every action that you take shall spread out and on for ever,
Affecting the whole of life.

‹ 128 ›

THERE came an oriental, who told me that his country had been ruined, and his people corrupted, by the influence of European civilisation.
I answered:
These are the reactions of life.
What seems to you painful, and which is indeed painful in a relative sense,
Is the travail of growth.
When the life of your people is so changed, that whatever is harmful in European ways, has no evil effect, and whatever is good is absorbed;
And when European civilisation is itself so modified, by its contacts with your own, that it ceases to be dangerous to itself or to you;

The present tension shall cease,
And you shall endue each other with new life.

⟨ 129 ⟩

A EUROPEAN told me that his land was polluted by the presence of coloured races.
I gave him a similar reply.

⟨ 130 ⟩

A DAY will come when men's food will be simple and clean, grown from the earth;
Vegetables, roots, cereals, nuts and fruit;
Raw often, with all their freshness and life;
Eaten mostly in the season and the climate which produced them;
Varying with temperaments and with tastes,
Yet ever chosen instinctively, without thought.

A day when the killing of animals,
The cleaning away of their bowels,
And the eating of their flesh,
Shall be held degrading;
To be avoided whenever possible.

⟨ 131 ⟩

I STAYED by one in sickness.
And it seemed to me that here the earth speaks clearly and directly;
With gentleness.

⟨ 132 ⟩
IN my heart lives the whole universe;
And in yours also.
So that I know you well; and, when we meet, we shall need no introduction.
For I knew you before you were born,
And shall know you also after you are dead.
Is there anyone in all the world, who knows you better?

⟨ 133 ⟩
I LIVE for ever in Paradise.
Nothing disturbs me; nothing surprises me.
I have that peace which passes knowledge,
Which is as a thing unknown;
Becoming the most certain thing on earth.

⟨ 134 ⟩
I HAVE no message that can convince;
No one to convert.
Only, I have understood something, concerning which I write.
Further, I know that my understanding will soon be given to many;
In the same way that the first men knew that their self-consciousness was not an illusion of their brains;
But the heritage of their race.

‹ 135 ›

THIS happened to me suddenly:
One day, as I walked in an eastern city,
My surroundings were lit as by an inward light.
And in that instant I knew in my mind, the workings of the universe;
Knew my place in it;
That I was immortal;
Without sin or fear of death.
I understood the meaning of life,
And my relationship to the earth.
I saw the heritage of man.

It is out of that experience, that I have written this book.

‹ 136 ›

I DRAW my understanding from the same source as that from which Lao Tse and Buddha and Christ and Mohammed drew theirs;
And I know it.
Nothing can dislodge that knowledge;
Nor can the death of my body destroy it.
For I know that in that understanding I am immortal;
I know that it resides in you, as it resides in me;
Awaiting its unfolding.
And I know that that inspiration cannot be communicated to you by any man, or religion, or philosophy.

It lies within you; and the hour of its awakening,
Is not of your choosing.

‹ 137 ›

I am God.
Within me burns a spark of Life,
Putting forth energy,
For ever and for ever.

‹ 138 ›

The consciousness which I have here described,
Is even now awakening in the minds of men.
It cannot be held back or suppressed;
No laws, no systems of government, no censor, nor the burning of books,
Can hold it in check.
Its coming is being unknowingly evolved by everything that exists.
Every effort to withhold it, strengthens its growth;
Every intelligent aid to it, is an act which so informs the stream of life,
As to have incalculable results.

‹ 139 ›

There are in you, as it were, two beings;
(Selves, forces, essences, existences—call them what you will.)

First, the spirit of the Universe, which brought you into
 being;
Which is the same in me, in everyone, in everything that is;
Through which you have identity with everything,
With the Universe itself.

Secondly, there is you;
A self-conscious, individual you;
Different in identity from everyone; different from me;
Acting, thinking, being—you;
Clothed in a body of your own;
The perfect expression of yourself.

When you bring these two selves into relation,
Then you are in heaven.

When the conscious motive of every deed and every
 thought is the motive of the Universe;
When every act is knowingly in accord with the purpose
 of the earth;
When the individual you is in harmony with the universal
 you;
Then indeed you have attained to wisdom,
And to peace.

‹ 140 ›

O LIFE, there is nothing in you that I have not known;
No joy, no happiness, no pain, no suffering, that has not
 been mine.

I have tasted each experience, and drunk of all your moods.
I come at last to know you, and to live.

O life, whose image I have written here;
O death, O love, I find myself in you.

‹ 141 ›

I passed by a thousand cemeteries.
And in one of them, I thought:
Some day, when men die, their bodies will be carried out
    in friendship,
To be buried in the open country,
That their substance may return to the earth,
To give forth beauty and new life,
In trees and herbs and flowers;
Which shall be deemed a fitting memorial.

Then these sad places shall be made gardens;
The stones uprooted and turned to noble use.

‹ 142 ›

The work of prostitutes, and the work of priests, is neces‑
    sary.
Yet if one profession be but a little older than the other,
So shall they both cease to exist about the same time.

As long as men shall make a mystery of God,
So long shall there be priests to minister to it.

As long as men shall make a mystery of their bodies, and
 of women's bodies,
So long shall there be prostitutes to save them from hell.

For the body of man, is the image of God;
And mystery is but the cloak of fear.
While man fears his body, or its parts, or its functions,
Prostitution shall flourish.
While man fears God, and His laws, and His punish‹
 ments,
Religion shall endure.

But when man comes to love and accept his body,
Prostitution shall cease.
And when man comes to love God,
Who is himself, and all mankind, and every living creature,
 and every plant, and tree, and the whole earth, and
 the universe,
There shall be no more priests.
And man shall no longer be an image of God;
He shall be God.

‹ 143 ›

Two men came to me with an argument about freedom,
 intuition and reason.
I said:
All existence is governed by the laws of existence.
In so far as you act in harmony with those laws,

You are free.
In so far as your actions fight against them,
You are bound.

Reason and intuition are, as it were, two channels connecting yourselves with the laws of life.
Their relative utility depends upon your capacity to keep them open.

⟨ 144 ⟩

THERE came a young man, who said:
Can you put me on the road that leads to the earth of your vision?
I answered:
Life is the road.   You are on it.
Accept all that life brings you;
Refuse nothing that life asks;
Pass nothing by in haste or in fear;
Enjoy to the full such pleasures as you meet;
And when the way comes difficult and dark,
Go on in faith.

⟨ 145 ⟩

SOME day education will be designed to encourage the unfettered growth of individuals;
To let them be themselves;
To give them the companionship, and the freedom,
Of the earth.

‹ 146 ›

THERE came a man who could find no good in life.
I said:
The psychologists believe that anyone who abuses life, is really stating his own dissatisfaction with himself.
So that when you tell me that the human race becomes more crapulous every minute,
I feel concerned for your welfare.
I, on the other hand, have discovered that the human race is faultless ; so you will understand how joyful I am;
And that I need not, after all,
Worry myself about you.

‹ 147 ›

AN engineer asked:
Is machinery good or bad ?
I answered :
Neither. Machines are in themselves soulless things, the inventions, and servants, of man.

If they are used for gain,
They shall help to enslave man;
To turn him into an automaton, forcing him to manufacture ever-increasing quantities of goods, aggravating the struggle for markets, intensifying commercial crises, swelling unemployment.

If they are used for love,
They shall help to make life gracious;
Adding to the power and to the dignity of man;
Harnessing the forces of nature to his use;
Giving him the freedom of the earth.

‹ 148 ›

Some day it will be known that to be ill is to be out of harmony with life;
And when sickness comes it will be treated with understanding;
The causes found and put away;
The results dispersed by natural means.
Then health will be the order of the day.

‹ 149 ›

One spoke to me of political systems.
I answered:
These institutions are like plants.
They shall flourish in their time, and when their time is done, they shall wither and die.
If they are cut back, they will grow more sturdily;
If they suppress other vital growths, they shall the more quickly perish.
For just as they supplanted the outgrown,
So shall they be supplanted.

The life of the earth inevitably unfolds;
No repressions or reactions shall retard it;
No unintelligent enthusiasms shall hasten it;
But all these together go to make up life.

⟨ 150 ⟩
I WAS asked whether the whole of mankind was destined to evolve into the people described in my vision.
I answered:
Not all, but a great number.
Yet this is a question about which you need not be concerned.
For it is a characteristic of every stage of evolution, that that part which moves onwards, is freed from the control of whatever remains;
And the parts that remain, rest content.
The trees are not subject to the mineral world;
Nor are the animals jealous of mankind.

Those who are satisfied with life, will retain their present state of consciousness;
Those who are unhappy, will progress.

⟨ 151 ⟩
A MAN spoke to me about psycho-analysis and psycho-synthesis.
I answered:

These are among the means by which man shall unveil
    himself to himself.
In their beginnings they are uncertain and misunderstood;
In their fulfilment they shall take their place, an honoured
    one,
Within the science of the earth.

⟨ 152 ⟩

A PHILOSOPHER said to me:
I seek to determine the laws of life;
Yet, in all these pages, I cannot encompass the truth.
I answered:
The gift of flowers is not wholly to the botanist;
But rather to the child, who crushing them within its arms,
Breathes in their life.

    The knowledge of men comes not to some surgeon,
        dissecting dead bodies,
    But to lovers.

    The laws of life shall not be determined by the friends of
        wisdom,
    But by those who live.

⟨ 153 ⟩

I CAME to a congress of young people,
Young men and women, full of creative energy.
They sang a lot of old songs,

And danced some medieval dances.
Then, their energies being spent in this pleasing and picturesque manner,
They went away,
Half satisfied.

‹ 154 ›

As I looked through a fashionable paper, it came to me that some day people would be more interested in their bodies than in clothes;
In the people round them, than in film stars;
In life, than in other folks' dances, garden parties or sport.

‹ 155 ›

SOMEONE spoke to me in a whisper about sex.
And someone else shouted to me in the street,
About Sex.

What is all this secrecy and blatancy and unhealth?
Are the animals furtive about sex, or absorbed in it?
Do they not make love in due season, openly and without shame?
When will man return to the same dignity?

When will the love of a man for a woman, or of a woman for a man,
Be esteemed a perfect thing?

And the love of a man for his comrade,
And of a woman for her friend, be blessed?

I tell you that in the heart of man, love takes the place of
 honour;
Gently, and without ceremony, she takes the place of
 honour.
Ponder on that, and all your questions about sex
Shall be answered.

‹ 156 ›

To a meeting of life reformers, I said:
If you mean your own lives, change is within the power of
 each of you.
If you mean my life, or someone else's life,
You might as well reform the sea;
It will escape you.

‹ 157 ›

I CAME to an art exhibition.
Room after room full of beauty;
Scenes so wonderful, so charged with the promise of life;
Yet, there was one thing lacking.

In all those halls, I did not see a single fine person.
There was a woman with one leg shorter than the other;
A second, whose stomach quivered like a mountain of
 jelly;

A listless guardian;
A youth with a red face and a blotched nose;
A tired student—resting;
And a man who carried in his manner all the importance of the earth.
No, though I stayed there for two hours, I did not see a single well-made person.

Outside there was a strapping workman, with laughing eyes.
He had no interest in art shows,
No cash to pay the entrance.
I enjoyed looking at him.

‹ 158 ›

It is not by building perfect houses, or by lying naked in the sun, or by eating wholesome food, that the millennium will come.
Nor yet by having perfect health, nor faultless education.
For all these things are effects as much as causes.
Indeed everything is perfect in its place and time,
Nor could exist outside its place and time.
Are not the very words—place and time—the co-ordinates by which everything in life is fixed?

‹ 159 ›

O you reformers of the world,
You who would change the earth by spreading some religion, or system of life,

Are your own hearts free?
Free from prejudice, ignorance, opinion?
Free from doubt, desire or fear?
Can you accept every thought of your own mind?
Every act of your own body?
Are you yourselves beautiful in everything you do and are?
Are you indeed Gods?

For I have heard a voice saying:
My earth is good.

⟨ 160 ⟩

A MAN asked me:
What is the object of life?
I answered:
That the spirit of life—the energy—which is the universe,
Which is in action in all things, following the rhythms of existence,
May become conscious.
That blind nature may see.

⟨ 161 ⟩

A WOMAN asked me:
What is the object of death?
I answered:
Re-birth; new life.

‹ 162 ›

I WALKED through the highway of a great city, looking at the shops, the houses and the traffic.
Of all that I saw there was nothing that had not been made by a simple working man or woman.
No masonry, no roof, no door, no window;
No motor-car, no merchandise, no pavement, no roadway;
Nor any tree that had not been planted by them.

Yet in all that street no working man or woman lived.
Nor did I see any sitting in the limousines;
Nor buying in the shops.
All was too fine for them.

Your work is not wasted.
Your heritage awaits the day when you are grown to enter into it.
And on that day, it shall not be withheld, even for an hour.
But if you snatch at it before the time, it shall wither in your hands;
To be slowly re-created.

‹ 163 ›

ALL growth is at once a progress and a retrogression.
The salts of the earth are absorbed by plants, to be turned to more complex compounds.
The plants are assimilated by animals and men, to be

transformed into organisms still more intricate in character.
When men die their bodies decompose into the simpler constituents that nourish plants.
And when the plants die, their components return to the simple salts of the earth.
So on, simultaneously, and always;
Following the rhythms of the seasons and the cycles of time.

And these transformations and reductions are brought about by the agency of lesser organisms, which are themselves subject to laws of progression and evolution.
Thus every phase of growth is interpenetrated by smaller, corresponding, or extended phases;
So that the growth and destruction of bodies is attended by conversions of spirit, of institutions, and by the evolution of forms.
And all these phases and growths and movements act and react upon each other, within the rhythms to which they relate;
From morning to evening, from summer to winter, from life to death, from civilisation to civilisation, from cycle to cycle;
To form a system so intricate as to be beyond the power of the intellect to encompass;
But which is held within the unknown regions of the soul.

‹ 164 ›

I GOT drunk.
And it seemed as if a door into heaven had opened,
And I partook of perfect happiness.

Only, in a little while,
Another door opened,
And I was thrown out.
My fall was so great that I cannot remember how it was with me there,
Nor tell you anything about it.

‹ 165 ›

LOOK at all these temples, cathedrals, castles, tombs.
If men do as much for an ideal that is far;
Do you think they will do less for reality, that is near?

And they have built these palaces for gold.
Do you think they will build less for love?

‹ 166 ›

MAN shall grow in accord with his reactions to the environment in which he is.
If circumstances force him in one direction, he shall grow in that direction;
If circumstances extinguish him, he shall be extinguished.

And it shall be an indication that his manner of growth
  in that time and place, was no longer in harmony with
  the scheme of things.
But grow he must;
For growth is the essence of life.

‹ 167 ›

To all the gentle saints who trod this earth,
To every warrior of truth and liberty,
I make a salutation.

I do not worship them;
For so I should deny the cause,
For which they lived.

‹ 168 ›

Beloved, I am near.
There is no veil can screen you from my eyes;
Nor anything in me to hide.

‹ 169 ›

While man seeks gain, he shall be subject to the laws of
  gain.
Factories shall arise in a moment,
And be deserted yet more quickly,
When they lose.
Cities shall spring up, and become desolate;

Harbours be built, railways constructed, mines sunk;
All for gain.

⟨ 170 ⟩

ONE asked me:
What are you trying to say?
I answered:
It is everything and it is nothing.
It is to go on living; which you will in any case do.
It is to tell you that there is something in life that is beneath
    the surface of appearances, and which you cannot see.
It is to say something that you cannot understand;
Which, if you could understand,
There would be no need to say.

⟨ 171 ⟩

AN enthusiast came to me, saying:
You have a message for the world.
I answered:
If I have, it is the same as the message of the grass, of the
    flowers and of the trees.
It has the same meaning as have the animals and man.
It is life, and the purpose of life;
Freedom, and the use of it;
Love.

It is the message of the earth, and of everything on the
    earth.
It is yours as well as mine.

‹ 172 ›
I MET a man who disliked politicians.
I said:
So long as man shall seek advantages for himself,
So long will he elect the politicians who promise him the most.
It matters nothing that such promises cannot be kept.
He will pay more attention to them than to the character of the man that makes them.

‹ 173 ›
ONE evening, I was taken to the room of a strangely happy youth.
To-morrow, he said, I know that I shall die.
Yet I do not fear death.
I fear rather the bestiality and the degradation of this life.
I have suffered greater torture than any death can hold.
I go out in peace and love and utter thankfulness.

At dawn, he was shot, for a coward.
So young, so brave, so unconcerned, he seemed.

‹ 174 ›
A MAN asked me if our civilisation would destroy itself.
I answered:
In a sense yes; in a sense no.
A civilisation based on gain is for ever destroying itself.
Out of it shall grow a civilisation based on love.

It will die, as a caterpillar dies,
To give birth to new life.

⟨ 175 ⟩

SOMEBODY spoke to me about different forms of government.
I answered:
All human institutions are the embodiment of the life which causes them.
The governments of the kings of long ago, were suitable to their day.
Existing governments are suitable to theirs.
As soon as they are out of tune with life,
They will be modified.

⟨ 176 ⟩

IF mankind does so much with half the world hating what it does, with enormous numbers idle, with every channel of activity restricted by the need of gain;
Do you think that mankind will do less when what is done, is done for love?
When all men create, when every channel is open and free?
Not less—but many times more.

⟨ 177 ⟩

THE school where you shall learn, is your present experience.
By it you shall grow.

If you run away from it, it will return to you.
But when you master it, it shall disappear.
Though you flee to the ends of the earth,
You cannot escape from yourself.

⟨ 178 ⟩

To a man of the west I said:
It is not sufficient to do.
To a man of the east I said:
It is not sufficient to know.
To a man of the south I said:
It is not sufficient to feel.

It suffices to be.
And the most perfect being,
Is he that knows and feels and acts,
To perfection.

⟨ 179 ⟩

WHILE the race grows to fulfilment,
Parts of it shall run to far extremes.
Hard-faced women, covered with furs and diamonds, living on cocktails;
Warped young men, crawling about, rotten with disease;
Self-satisfied people; deluded people;
Emaciated wretches, covered with vermin and sores, scrabbling through rubbish for trifles;
Ardent fanatics, sacrificing everything, even life, for their desire;

Arrogant bosses, thrusting aside all opposition, tyrannical and sure;
Meek, self-effacing people.

But all, however grotesque, shall putrefy in time;
Out of them shall grow forms of life of greater simplicity;
And life cannot grow otherwise.

‹ 180 ›

IN the year of the great war, man began to expend energy in unproductive purposes, at the rate of about twenty million pounds' worth a day.
Man kept that up for four years, and was not exhausted.
Since then, man has increased in number, and far more power has been harnessed to his use.
Do you think that it will take him long to turn this world into a wondrous place,
Once his heart is set upon it?
A world of gracious fields and cities, of good communications;
A world where everyone shall receive full measure of the necessities of life, of beauty and of truth.

Once his heart is set upon it.

‹ 181 ›

A LADY told me of her loneliness.
I answered:

Is it not because you cut yourself off from everyone else?
Firstly, you are white; and you feel yourself superior to all coloured people. That separates you from three-fourths of the world.
Secondly, you consider your nation to be above the other white nations; thus dividing yourself from nine-tenths of the remainder.
Then you are a lady, and cannot mix with the lower classes.
Again, your political and religious views are such that you do not wish to associate with fools or bigots.
And of the people nearest to you, some are selfish or careless in their habits, or difficult to do anything with;
While the rest are occupied in affairs.
And you cannot be bothered with affairs.

⟨ 182 ⟩

WHEN I listened to the drums of Africa,
It seemed to me that here music had remained pure rhythm;
As it were an empty vehicle, waiting to be filled,
With the power, and with the meaning, of life.

⟨ 183 ⟩

Do you imagine that any particular individual is more important to the earth than another?
Or that any tree is more important than another?
Or any insect more important than another?

Do you realise that no man could exist without other men, or without the trees, or without animals, or without insects, or even without microbes and bacteria?
His life depends upon them all.

‹ 184 ›

I CAME to a meeting of the youth of the world.
I said:
The brotherhood of man exists; it has existed as long as man.
The realisation of it arises from time to time in individuals.
It is a flame that burns unseen in the deepest recesses of hearts.
You can feed that flame which is in you; but you cannot feed it in others.
You may realise brotherhood and live accordingly;
But no society, no system, no example, no lecture, no book,
Will bring you to it.

‹ 185 ›

ONE said:
You have spoken of the greed of gain.
Is it not right that man should gain?
I answered:
It is more even than right; it is vital, inevitable.
It is the very means by which man discovers himself.
Gain—not only of wealth, but of power, fame, love, ease,

Nevertheless, when man has found himself, the fear of being deprived of any of these things shall drop off from him, as it were an outworn garment;
And love will become the motive of life.

‹ 186 ›

A YOUTH said to me:
The love of my body is for men, and not for women.
I answered:
Earth fashions our hearts to fill her needs.
Does the lily repine that it is not a rose?
Or the palm tree envy the oak?
Accept yourself, even as these accept;
And great shall be your understanding;
Vast the interpretations that you shall make.

‹ 187 ›

A STUDENT asked me the cause and the purpose of sexual inversion.
I answered:
All life is growth;
All growth, subject to change.
When a change of growth is in process, nature restricts the expenditure of creative energy in one direction,
To promote it in another.
The effect on the unit of life concerned is to occasion a state of tension, of distress,
Followed by a change of growth.

Sexual inversion is a re-direction of creative energy, attended by suffering, and followed by evolution.

The same is true of unemployment, war, illness, and of all other states of tension or suffering, in which man, both collectively and individually, finds himself.

And the same is true of death.

‹ 188 ›

I CAME to a meeting of engineers.
I said:
Of all the great undertakings which you construct;
Of everything that helps man, that lessens his burdens;
There will remain a gift to life.

But everything which you invent to aid man to torture himself,
Shall be destroyed.

‹ 189 ›

THE body of man is greater than any work of art;
More beautiful than any painting;
More wonderful than any building;
More useful than any machine;
More eloquent than words;
Finer than music.

‹ 190 ›
Pain is the sign of growth.
Yet there is no virtue in suffering for suffering's sake.
He therefore that seeks pain, indulges himself;
He that understands it, is in the way of truth;
And he that is beyond it, is near to God.

‹ 191 ›
I am not offering you consolation, or an easy path to heaven,
    or any secret formula by which you can get happiness,
    or gain anything for yourself.
On the contrary—I am informing you that you will have
    none of these things,
Until your self has been laid aside.

‹ 192 ›
A man said to me:
You cannot change human nature.
I answered:
I have no wish to.
Human nature changes itself.

‹ 193 ›
I tell nothing in confidence.
I shout as loud as I can.
Yet, if what I say means nothing to you,
It is as if I had been silent.

‹ 194 ›

A YOUNG man came running with the news of five sailors,
   drowned slowly in a submarine.
He asked: Is it enough?
I answered:
It is not.
Not five, nor five thousand, nor five million, shall be
   enough to change the world;
Be they the finest and the strongest of young men;
Be they slowly suffocated through nights and days;
Be they torn limb from limb by shell fire, and their entrails
   scattered;
Lie they groaning for hours till freed by death.
It is not enough even for you;
For if your heart were changed, you would not come running to me.
As to the rest, their hearts are not in your care;
Nor in mine.
And they shall build many submarines, and worse;
And many of the youth of the world shall die in agony;
That, in the end, man may learn freedom.

‹ 195 ›

CAN you see the whole world flouting death, and yet,
   with a calm mind, do your work in peace?
Can you understand the perfection of growth?
Can you accord that same liberty to others, which you seek
   for yourself?

Can you live and enjoy every moment, observing all
    things, thinking and making conclusions?
Can you unveil every mystery; even, and especially, the
    mystery of your own mind?

‹ 196 ›

I saw an old young lady playing patience;
Playing patience while the world went round;
Playing it while somewhere in the east a robber had his
    head chopped off;
While somewhere in the south, a girl was being taught to
    love;
While somewhere in the west, a man tried hard to
    think.

‹ 197 ›

I came to a great exhibition.
Tired, so tired, I walked for miles,
Among the palaces of people who had things to sell.
At last I came to a smiling negress proffering cigarettes,
And I smiled at her.

‹ 198 ›

A man spoke to me of evolution and revolution.
I answered:
The earth evolves unceasingly.
If the evolution of any part of it be hastened or retarded,

The forces underlying it gather strength, and in the end, burst their bonds.
That is called revolution.

‹ 199 ›

THERE will come a day when men will be free from the necessity of doing good works;
When they will be able to act in the understanding of God,
Rather than spend their time compensating themselves for their own limitations,
By trying to improve others.

‹ 200 ›

I AM in Hell.
Drop by drop, my blood has been pressed out, until my body dies;
Thought by thought, my mind has been destroyed, till no desire is left;
Phase by phase, has darkness overcome my soul; until,
I am in Heaven.

‹ 201 ›

THERE came many who were unhappy, seeking comfort.
I said to them:
If you are discontented or depressed, it is because you are out of harmony with the world you live in.
That world you cannot greatly alter.

Yet, by as much as you are able to grow into harmony with
 your surroundings,
To accord yourself to earth's song,
So will your pain grow less.

But remember that earth's song is a living thing.
Even as we speak, I hear its sound come clearer;
Even in our time, I feel its rhythm change;
And the hectic life of these days,
The rattle and nerve-rack and speed,
Dissolve into calm sweet notes of freedom;
The dawn of wisdom—Peace.

⟨ 202 ⟩

War.
O healing, cleansing war.
You fever of the nations, that sweeps away the poisons of
 the earth;
Making men clear of purpose, to give their hearts and
 souls and bodies wholly to the work in hand.
Bloody work;
Done in faith, in the comradeship of men.
Fearless men, and strong,
Sacrificing all in this;
Frightened men, and set;
Raising courage enough, till death or madness intervene;
Cursing men, and maimed;
Groaning, bleeding, wrecks.

Someday, O war, your fierceness shall become so great,
That men shall seek the poison upon which you thrive,
To end its brewing;
And you shall be destroyed.

⟨ 203 ⟩

LIFE is like a great and intricate machine, filling hall after hall.
And there are many who run at it, saying:
This wheel turns too slowly, or too fast.
And they push or pull, without any grand result.
But there are a few who are able to contemplate it as a whole; who study it and know it; and who can, by some small action, timed to perfection, exert an immeasurable influence.
And when you realise that the machine covers acres and acres, that it is in fact the whole earth,
You will understand the difficulty of seeing it complete.
And if it should come to you to know that you are yourself a little wheel in that machine,
Perhaps it might seem to you that the best work which you can do for life
Is to function perfectly in your appointed place
Until life comes to rest.

⟨ 204 ⟩

THE priests of one religion were denied wives;
And of another, wine;

Of yet another, tobacco;
Another, meat; another, war.

Yet I heard a pacifist minister cursing his wife.
And I saw a non-smoker being very drunk.
I knew a mullah, abstainer from alcohol, who ate too
    well;
And a celibate priest who loved a boy.

So that it seemed as if old nature
Sometimes laughed at the laws of God.

⟨ 205 ⟩

To a meeting of earth improvers, I said:
You see life as a river;
And you would straighten its course, remove rocks, bring
    calm to troubled places,
And make it into a respectable smooth-running stream.

All that is maya; illusion.
You are yourselves drops of water within the river of
    life;
And your power to change life's flow,
Is comparable to the power of a drop of water in a
    river
To change that river's course.

But you can change yourselves.

‹ 206 ›

Life will not stand still.
The most quiescent races in the world shall struggle and
    seethe,
As in the East;
Or perish,
As in the South Sea Isles.

The most unwise nations shall destroy each other,
As in Europe;
Or learn wisdom.

‹ 207 ›

Can you carve out of life, solidly and for all time, that
    which your heart desires?
Can you accept every experience, drawing from it what
    virtue it possesses?
Can you follow your genius to the end of time and beyond;
    to create and create and create?

You are indeed a God.

‹ 208 ›

One came asking for consolation.
I answered:
There is only one kind of consolation that is permanent.
Of the temporary sorts there are many, bottled and other‑
    wise;

But their effect is often ugly, and in any case wears off.
You shall not be wholly and finally satisfied,
Until you find yourself.

⟨ 209 ⟩

I WAS asked the meaning of illness.
I answered:
To have perfect health, is to live in perfect harmony with life;
To have the work and rest, food and thoughts, recreation and environment, which are most suitable to your state;
And to be able instinctively to change these things, in accord with the changes of life.
But to fail in any of this, is to induce a condition of disease, of illness, of unhealth,
Which shall itself tend to correct the want of harmony
That is its cause.

Further, there are some conditions of life which are in themselves so discordant, that it is hard for the people who are forced to endure them to live in health.
Conditions of ill-housing, of insanitation, of poisoned atmosphere, of unhealthy work and food, of the presence of venomous beasts and disease-bearing insects, of blind education, and of untruthful propaganda.

LIFE

These shall remain sores upon the face of the earth,
Until mankind has the energy, and the ability, to correct them.
And the health of all men who are forced into these conditions shall suffer;
Producing, as it were, an illness of society;
Which also shall tend to correct the want of harmony
That is its cause.

⟨ 210 ⟩

MANY discussed with me the institutions, practices and phases of life.
In each case I felt that we were but stating and analysing the reactions of self-seeking to self-seeking, and of life to life;
That while these were matters which we might discuss, they were beyond our control;
That we could but modify our own reactions to them, and to life as a whole;
And that they, the institutions, practices and phases of life, would themselves change,
As we changed.

For every system produces the reactions necessary to its own growth, modification and absorption
Into the life of the earth;
Giving place to new forms,
As time goes on.

⟨ 211 ⟩

A DAY will come when the teachers in schools will all be men and women who love children, and have faith in them.

Masters who ever renew their genius, changing their methods as inspiration comes, refusing to crystallise into moulds.

The most creative in action,

The most free in mind,

The most joyful in heart.

And the schools will all vary in character; following the diversities of feeling of the pupils, the teachers and the parents.

But all will give happiness to children.

⟨ 212 ⟩

THESE things I promise you:

Firstly; that every experience, every pain, and suffering, shall be removed as soon as you have learnt its lesson.

Secondly; no suffering shall come to you that is too hard for you to bear.

So that if you can hold on in faith

You shall win through in peace.

⟨ 213 ⟩

You shall seek wealth, or knowledge, or fame;

Health, perfection, or ease;

Work, or virtue; love, or respectability;

Or salvation,
Or escape from boredom,
Or self-expression.
You cannot stay inert.
The energy that is within you cannot remain at rest.
And in seeking, you shall find yourself.

⟨ 214 ⟩

A LADY asked me:
Are you against marriage?
I answered:
To everything, I am indifferent.
So long as marriage is necessary to people, they will marry.
It will give them a measure of security, and the respect of their neighbours.
But such a state will not always be ranked higher than love in freedom.
For a merchant, who deals fairly, without a written contract,
Is not thought less worthy than one who holds to legal forms;
And to desire the respect of neighbours, often leads to dullness and deceit.
Further, the measure of protection given by bonds,
Is equal to the loss of liberty.

⟨ 215 ⟩

ARGUMENTS do not alter facts.
In the end love—nature—earth—wisdom—shall prevail.

If you look out of the window of your mind, you will see
    nature growing, growing.
It is the same now, or in a thousand years.
All your laws and theories, ideas and arguments,
Must give place to that fact.

< 216 >

O THE joy of success;
To see work breeding—energy and profits growing.
The losing oneself in busy industry, activity, results.
For what?

O the joy of creation;
The world of one's dreams taking shape under one's eyes
    and hands;
The giving birth to art.
For what?

O the satisfaction of possession;
To have all one wants; property, beauty, power.
For what?

O the joy of love;
To hold within one's arms, a friend.
For what?

To give them all back again?
To have done with them in the end?
To endure the pain of loss, the sorrow of doubt?

For none of these;
But to learn the joy of life.

‹ 217 ›

Can you take all life with both arms, and be free?
Can you be humble and meek and patient and untiring?
Can you persevere, without regard to my promises, or to anyone's promises?
Can you keep pace with the earth?
Can you wait?

‹ 218 ›

Can you set your face to the wind, and fight and strive for truth?
Can you earn wealth and spend it for life's sake?
Can you give up everything, even life itself?
Can you learn to accept everything; to find nothing ugly or indecent, or unnecessary?
Can you lay bare your own soul, and not shudder at the sight?

‹ 219 ›

I passed through sickness and despair,
And utter loneliness.

‹ 220 ›

There is no sin which I have not committed;
No crime, of which I have not been guilty.

And at some time or other, I have sold my mind, as well
    as my body;
Like everyone else.

⟨ 221 ⟩

Then, when I had lived through all experience,
I came at last into these hills—to be alone—to put all in
    order;
To take out from these pages,
Hate, scorn, bias, fear;
To weave into them, if it might be,
Truth.

⟨ 222 ⟩

Old Earth,
You whom I have here described and laughed at;
Analysed and lived on, loved and walked upon;
You are perfect.
There is nothing in you which I can, or would, transform.
You will go on changing yourself, growing up, filling each
    hour with life;
Every moment of you faultless and complete.
While I, who indeed belong to you
Watch, and am content.

IV

THE STORY OF THE EARTH

THE STORY OF THE EARTH

Throughout—beyond—Existence,
I feel the ageless universe ;
Worlds within worlds—moving in rhythm—
    time without time ;
Complete in itself,
Held now in a unit of life, and knowing itself held
Still—here for ever perfect,
Singing a song.

THE STORY OF THE EARTH

⟨ 1 ⟩
BEYOND Time—the unknowable.

⟨ 2 ⟩
OUT of the unknown grew this universe;
These suns and stars and worlds.
Our Earth; a particle, a phase, a reflection of that;
In endless time.

⟨ 3 ⟩
IN the beginning the earth was fire, pure energy,
A whirling radiance, subject to the sun.

⟨ 4 ⟩
TIME passed: millions of millions of years.
Energy was caught into form; the reaction of force upon force:
Gases, liquids, solids;
Air, water, earth.
The minerals crystallised into being.

⟨ 5 ⟩
TIME passed: thousands of millions of years.
Form acquired growth; the reaction of matter to matter:

The beginnings of animal and vegetable life;
The movements of living bodies.

‹ 6 ›

TIME passed: hundreds of millions of years.
Into growth dawned consciousness; the reaction of life upon life;
Beasts and birds and fishes, having minds and instincts,
Fighting for preservation.

‹ 7 ›

TIME passed: millions and millions of years.
Consciousness awakened into self-consciousness; the reaction of mind upon mind:
Man, knowing himself alive, talking, working, thinking, inventing,
Striving to find the truth, seeking himself.

‹ 8 ›

TIME passed: hundreds of thousands of years;
Until now.
Self-consciousness becomes illuminated by universal being; the reaction of self-seeking to self-seeking.
And man draws near to that peace and wisdom in which he shall know the meaning of existence, and of his relationship to life;
In which he shall acquire the certainty of immortality;
In which he shall find himself free from sin,

Free from the bonds of self-seeking;
In which he shall inherit the earth,
And become one with God.

‹ 9 ›

TIME will pass: unnumbered years.
Earth, alive in the consciousness of man,
Shall go on in joy and gladness,
Towards the unknown.
And beyond it—the timeless unknowable.

.   .   .   .   .

This is the story of the Earth, relative to Time.

‹ 10 ›

WITHIN that relationship, there exist innumerable other worlds;
Whose energies inform the earth, or are informed by it;
Whose growths contain it, or are contained in it;
Whose beings are consummated within it, or whose consummation
Earth portends.

‹ 11 ›

WITHOUT that relationship,
There are phases of existence,
Whose significance is not reflected in the mirror of Time;
Which it is hard for the mind to know.

‹ 12 ›

This is the story of the Earth.
It consents the truest findings of philosophy, of religion and of science.
It keeps faith with man.

‹ 13 ›

This is the story of the Earth.
It is written in your heart
And in Life.

‹ 14 ›

READ.

About the Author

Frank Townshend lived in England from 1887 to 1974. He attended the Royal Military Academy as a young man, was commissioned into the Royal Engineers in 1906, and was promoted to Lieutenant in 1908. He eventually became a Captain and served in World War I in France with the Field Army for most of the war. He was awarded the Military Cross and Croix de Chevalier in early 1916, and finally left the Army in 1926. All that is known of him beyond this is that he was an author, poet and artist who studied at Ecole Julien in Paris, lived in India for a while, contributed articles to Theosophist and Buddhist magazines, and remained unmarried.

He wrote five books titled *Earth* (1929), *Heaven* (1930), *Becoming* (1939), *Amen* (1952) and *Hell* (1955). His books are considered amazing and life-changing for most who read them. For example, his book *Earth* inspired a choral symphony called "Vision of the Earth," and one book reviewer said, "This may be the most important book ever written about mankind and our relationship to all things. Part philosophy, part religion, part poetry, the book is an observation of mankind and how we have evolved over history into what we are and what our lives are today. No author has ever summarized humanity as correctly as Frank Townshend. It's the closest to a comprehensive understanding of the totality of existence as we can have in print." Few people know of his work, so The Book Tree is the only publisher to find his first two titles and bring them back into print. We hope to reprint them all, if found, so that his work will not be forgotten.